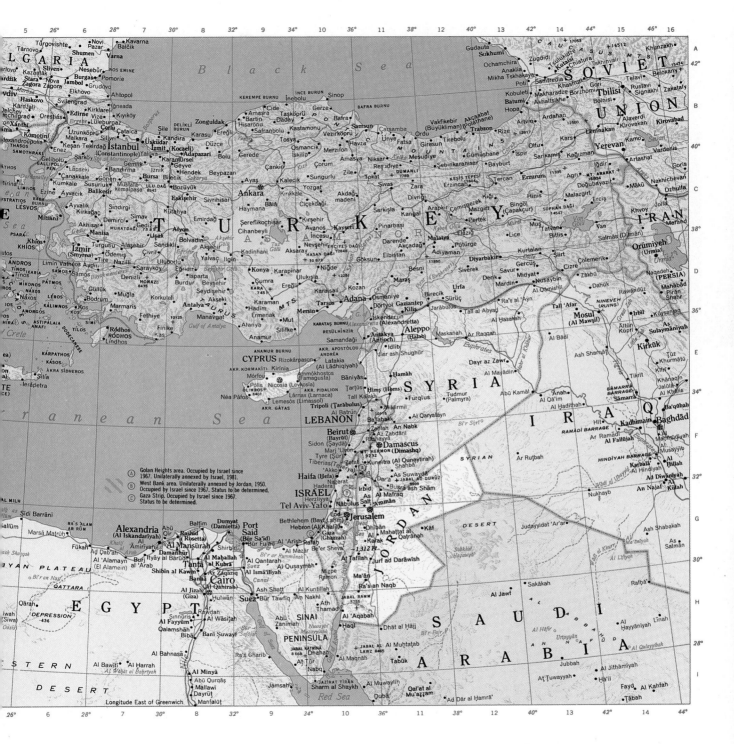

Enchantment of the World

JORDAN

By Leila Merrell Foster

Consultant for Jordan: Timothy J. Piro, Ph.D. Candidate, Department of Political Science, George Washington University, Washington, D.C.

Consultant for Reading: Robert L. Hillerich, Ph.D., Visiting Professor, University of South Florida; Consultant, Pinellas County Schools, Florida

CHILDRENS PRESS®

CHICAGO

The ancient city of Petra

Library of Congress Cataloging-in-Publication Data

Foster, Leila Merrell.
 Jordan / by Leila M. Foster.
  p.   cm. — (Enchantment of the world)
 Includes index.
 Summary: Introduces the geography, history,
government, religion and culture of Jordan.
  ISBN 0-516-02603-8
  1. Jordan—Juvenile literature. [1. Jordan.]
I. Title. II. Series.
DS153.F67 1991   91-8888
956.95—dc20   CIP
                                                  AC

4 5 6 7 8 9 10 11 12 13 R 02 01 00 99 98 97 96

Picture Acknowledgments
AP/Wide World Photos: 6 (top left, center left, center
middle, center right), 46 (right), 47, 51, 54 (2 photos), 55,
59, 61 (right), 63, 66, 67, 87, 95
The Bettmann Archive: 18 (left), 28 (right), 31 (right), 32,
35 (2 photos), 36 (right), 37, 42 (2 photos), 44 (2 photos),
48, 49 (left)
© **Virginia R. Grimes:** 8 (left), 25, 99 (bottom right)
Historical Pictures Service, Chicago: 36 (left)

Journalism Services: © Fotex/H. Tschanz-Hofman, 9, 110
(top); © F. Giaccone, 101
North Wind Picture Archives: 28 (left), 31 (left)
Odyssey/Frerck/Chicago: © Robert Frerck, 27
Photri: 4, 10, 11 (right), 13, 22, 75 (2 photos), 80, 85 (2
photos), 86, 112, 113, 114 (2 photos), 116 (left)
© **Carl Purcell:** 5
Reuters/Bettmann Newsphotos: 6 (top right), 69, 70
H. Armstrong Roberts, Inc.: 117; © Geopress, 15, 38, 82,
116 (right)
Royal Jordanian Airlines: 90
SuperStock International, Inc.: 74, 108; © Ray Manley, 8
(right); © Herbert Lanks, 16 (bottom left); © Leonard Lee
Rue, 16 (top left); © Charles Bear, 20; © Tom Rosenthal,
21; © Hubertus Kanus, 34, 78 (left), 94 (left), 115; © Ace
Williams, 81, 94 (right); © John Bonar, 100; © G. Ricatto,
106 (bottom left); © Charles May, 107
TSW-CLICK/Chicago: © David Hanson, Cover; © Andy
Chadwick, 11 (left); © Nabeel Turner, 76; © Don Smetzer,
79 (right), 102 (right), 109
UPI/Bettmann Newsphotos: 6 (bottom), 24, 30, 46 (left),
49 (right), 57, 58, 61 (left), 64
Valan: © Christine Osborne, 6 (top center), 12, 19, 78
(right), 79 (left), 92, 94 (center top and bottom), 97, 99 (left
and top right), 102 (left and center), 103, 104, 106 (top and
bottom right), 110 (bottom); © Jeff Foott, 16 (top right); ©
Richard T. Nowitz, 17, 18 (right)
Len W. Meents: Maps on 105, 109, 112, 115
**Courtesy Flag Research Center, Winchester,
Massachusetts 01890:** Flag on back cover
Cover: Jordan, Petra, The Treasury, Bedouin on camel in
foreground

A Bedouin with his camel

TABLE OF CONTENTS

King Hussein, who rules Jordan as a constitutional monarch, is married to American-born Queen Noor. When he is not occupied with the business of Jordan, he enjoys spending time with his children, participating in sports, and flying airplanes.

Chapter 1

THE HASHEMITE
KINGDOM OF JORDAN

What nation is new, yet old? What country has a king who is a world leader and also a pilot, a sports car racer, a motorcyclist, a parachutist, a horseman, a hunter, a deep-sea fisherman, a water-skier, and a scuba diver? What land has a hidden city that has been thought to contain great treasure? The Hashemite Kingdom of Jordan is the answer to these questions.

Jordan is both new and old. The nation gained its independence in 1946, yet Jordan is the land of some of the oldest human settlements and of many of the stories in the Bible.

King Hussein rules Jordan as a constitutional monarch. He is the head of state and a world leader whose advice is sought. He has survived more than eleven assassination attacks. His responsibilities have not dampened his enthusiasm for sports of many kinds. He is a member of the Hashemite family that traces its ancestry to Muhammad, the prophet of the Islamic religion.

Jordan has many significant ruins of ancient civilizations. Petra, in the south of the country, is hidden away and must be approached by a narrow gorge. Travelers visiting the ruins may still ride in on horses or donkeys. In ancient times, the city had

One way to reach Petra is through the siq *(above), a narrow route through a sandstone canyon. The Treasury (right), which served as a tomb, is carved out of the rock. People once thought pirates hid their treasure here and so it is called the Treasury.*

a building called the Treasury, because people thought that one of the stone decorations contained an immense fortune.

The name "Jordan" comes from the Arabic word *Al Urdun*. It is an ancient expression for the Jordan River and the surrounding territory. The river flows from Mount Hermon in the north on the boundary between Lebanon and Syria to the Dead Sea. The land on the west side of the Jordan River and the Dead Sea is called the West Bank and the land on the east, the East Bank. In the short distance of about 100 air miles (161 kilometers) from its source at about 9,000 feet (2,743 meters) above sea level, the Jordan River drops to almost 1,300 feet (396 meters) below sea level where it enters the Dead Sea. The Dead Sea is the deepest depression on the land surface of our planet.

Jordan, in the southwestern part of Asia, borders Israel to the west, Syria to the north, Iraq to the east, and Saudi Arabia to the

A beach on the Gulf of Aqaba

southeast and the south. A port in the south on the Gulf of Aqaba gives Jordan access to the Red Sea. Many of the borders in the desert to the east do not follow any natural boundaries but are straight lines down from one point to another. To the west, the armistice line is the longest boundary of an Arab nation with Israel. Under the United Nations Armistice Agreement of April 3, 1949, Jordan was left in control of the West Bank. However, the Israelis occupied that territory in the war of 1967. In 1988 King Hussein severed legal and administrative ties with the West Bank in favor of the establishment of a Palestinian state under the leadership of the Palestine Liberation Organization (PLO). Palestinians are Arabs who lived on the land that was divided into Jordan and Israel in 1948.

Following the separation of the West Bank, the territory of Jordan remains about 35,000 square miles (90,650 square

The Jordan River

kilometers) and has a population of about 3.8 million. That makes Jordan about the size of Portugal, or the state of Kansas.

Most Jordanians are Arabs, and Arabic is the official language. English is understood by many people because that language is taught in most of Jordan's primary and secondary schools.

Jordan is an Islamic country; about 95 percent of the population is Sunni Muslim. There are small minorities of Christians and Shiite Muslims.

FROM MOUNTAINS TO THE DESERTS TO THE SEA

Several different kinds of land are found in Jordan. The great desert to the east takes up about four-fifths of the nation's territory. The Jordan River Valley is part of the great African Rift Valley, and then there are the East Bank Uplands.

Tourists often travel by camel (above) to see the desert scenery (left) of the Wadi Rum. Some of this landscape was filmed in the movie Lawrence of Arabia.

The desert areas to the east are on a plateau that tips slightly toward the west. The plateau is made up of ancient rocks covered by layers of newer rocks such as limestone. In the north, lava and basaltic rock cover the area. In the south there are outcrops of sandstone and granite that are worn down from wind erosion. Especially in the south, there are sand dunes and salt flats. Some of this landscape was filmed in the movie *Lawrence of Arabia*.

The East Bank Uplands tower anywhere from 2,000 feet to 5,750 feet (609 meters to 1,753 meters) over the Rift Valley. Here there are outcrops of sandstone, chalk, limestone, and flint. Wadis (stream beds that are dry most of the year except during the winter rains) cut across from the west; they create deep canyons that make travel difficult. The land is divided by these wadis into four districts that can be identified roughly with Old Testament kingdoms: Ajlun between the Yarmouk River and the Wadi Zarqa

Salt-encrusted rocks on the shore of the Dead Sea

(Gilead), Balqa between Zarqa and Mujib (part of Moab and the
territory of the Ammonities), Kerak from Wadi Mujib to Wadi
Hasa (Moab), and Ma'an from the Wadi Hasa to the Gulf of
Aqaba.

The Great Rift on the western boundary of Jordan extends from
Turkey in Asia to Tanzania in Africa. It is a great crack, or
depression, in the earth thought to be formed by two continental
plates moving sideways to each other. In the Jordan Valley that
movement is estimated to have been about fifty miles (eighty
kilometers). Earthquakes or tremors in the region have been
frequent; the last major one occurred in 1927. Lava flows resulting
from the movement of the earth's crust have made cultivation of
the land impossible in places. A small lava flow blocked the
waters of the River Jordan to form Lake Tiberias (the Sea of

The King's Highway twists and turns as it travels through the Jordan Valley.

Galilee). The Dead Sea, a salty lake with no outlet, is the lowest spot on the land area of the earth. South from the Dead Sea, the Wadi Araba continues in the depression until it reaches the Gulf of Aqaba.

The port of Aqaba has been an important trading post in ancient times and today. During the Iran-Iraq War in the 1980s it was used to ship war supplies to Iraq. The tip of the southern boundary provides Jordan with its only access to the sea. The deserts of Jordan have been a barrier to travel from the east to the Mediterranean Sea. The route up through the Jordan Valley, called the King's Highway, is one of the paths throughout history that has connected the lands of the Nile River to those of the Euphrates and Tigris rivers.

CLIMATE

Jordan has a rainy season from November to March with hot and dry weather for the rest of the year. Although the country does not touch the Mediterranean Sea, the climate is affected by that body of water as well as by altitude. Down near the Dead Sea, below sea level, the mean monthly temperatures range between 61 degrees Fahrenheit and 90 degrees Fahrenheit (16 degrees Celsius and 32 degrees Celsius). At Amman, the capital that is 2,362 feet (720 meters) above sea level, temperatures range from 44 degrees Fahrenheit to 87 degrees Fahrenheit (7 degrees Celsius to 31 degrees Celsius). At the beginning of the dry season, a hot wind called the *khamsin* blows from the south and the southeast. During the period from June to September, a wind called the *shamal* blows from the north and northeast. While the heat is extreme during the daytime, it cools after sunset. The prevailing wind is westerly to southwesterly. In the north there is more humidity.

Rainfall in a desert area is all-important for the growing of crops. During the short winter season, the rainfall may reach sixteen inches (forty-one centimeters) in the north, four inches (ten centimeters) in the south, and only two inches (five centimeters) out in the desert. Occasionally, the uplands may receive snow or frost.

VEGETATION AND WILDLIFE

At one time, forests and wooded areas covered the more mountainous parts of the country that received more rainfall. However, humans have cut down the trees and the soil has been carried away through erosion. As a result, the water table has

The springtime blossoms of an almond tree

been lowered. By the middle of the twentieth century the great forests had all but disappeared. Efforts at reforestation are being made. Trees such as pines, acacias, oaks, and cypress can be found in very small groves or standing alone. Grasses that die off in the summer heat are common. In the drier sections, sagebrush is the main plant. Shrubs with thorns abound. In the grasslands, lotus fruit and pistachios are found. Bright pink oleander bushes bloom in the spring along the wadis and rivers.

Even in a country that is drab during the rest of the year, spring rains bring out an amazing blossoming of flowers. Then lupins, tulips, cyclamens, daisies, irises, and even wild orchids bloom.

Jordan is one of the territories over which migratory birds fly between Europe and Africa. Both waterfowl and land birds can be counted—especially the stork. The golden eagle and the vulture

Golden eagles (top left) are found in Jordan. Leopards (above) and scorpions (left) also inhabit the region.

inhabit the region. Game birds that are found throughout the year where water is available are partridges, woodcocks, pigeons, quail, and grouse.

A surprising number of wild animals make Jordan their home. Ibex, gazelles, and antelope are found in the desert and around human habitations. Foxes, jackals, wolves, rabbits, hares, mongooses, and mole rats have been counted. In the more remote areas, wildcats such as panthers or leopards are sighted occasionally. South of the Dead Sea, wild boar are hunted.

Centipedes, scorpions, and several kinds of lizards also inhabit the country. Several types of poisonous snakes must be guarded against, and the levant viper, which hunts at night, is found even in inhabited regions.

Camels with their young

CAMELS AND HORSES

Perhaps the most intriguing animals in Jordan are the camel and the Arabian horse.

Camels carry great loads on their backs. They are ideally suited for transportation in the desert. They have been called "ships of the desert," "God's gift," and "God's bad joke."

Camels are thought to have originated in North America. One branch of the camel family that migrated into South America evolved into llamas, vicunas, and alpacas. Others crossed over into Asia by the Alaskan land bridge. Some developed two humps, the larger Bactrian camels that are found mostly in Siberia and China. The one-humped dromedaries kept migrating, on into Arabia and eventually into Africa.

A camel's large feet can handle hot and shifting sand, and its tough lips allow it to eat rough desert plants.

The Jordanian dromedary weighs about 1,400 to 1,600 pounds (635 to 726 kilograms). It measures 7 to 9 feet (2 to 2.7 meters) high up to the shoulders, with another foot (.3 meters) to the top of the hump. It has large feet that are suited for walking on hot and shifting sand. Two rows of eyelashes keep out sand during windstorms and cut down on sun glare. Also protection against sandstorms is the camel's ability to close up its ears, mouth, and nose. Tough lips make it possible for it to eat cacti and to nibble off the thorns and barbs of other plants.

In the desert, the camel's ability to go without food for several days and without water for much longer is an important asset. The food that is eaten passes through four different stomachs in the animal. When the camel does drink at a water hole, it will take in gallons of water. The camel does not sweat and passes off little of the water; body heat is reflected to some extent. The fat that is stored in the hump is available to the animal for use when food is not.

Members of the Jordanian Desert Patrol

The camel's disposition, however, is not appreciated by all, and there is a strong odor about a camel. The animal often will turn on even the person who feeds and waters it. The camel can aim quite well when spitting. Moreover, the camel may have different ideas than the rider about what to do. Getting on and off the camel is accomplished while the animal is squatting on the ground. Since the back end of the camel gets up first, the rider must have a firm grasp on the saddle and lean back. To dismount, the rider must be prepared for the front end of the animal going down first to the squatting position. There is a definite sway to the camel's gait as it moves both its right legs first and then the left ones.

Yet what a beautiful sight it is to see fine riders handle their camels. Several hundreds of the elite troops of the Jordanian Desert Patrol ride camels that are ideal mounts for tracking people in the desert—especially the smugglers who may be trying to bring in illegal goods to Jordanian markets.

An Arabian stallion

The Bedouin, the inhabitants of the desert areas, can use the camel for meat and milk. The hair of the camel can be made into clothes and tents. Dried dung is used for fuel. The camel is an ideal carrier of goods and humans in desert areas.

Arabian horses long have been admired throughout the world for beauty, intelligence, and stamina. The Bedouin value the endurance of the horse most, while Europeans emphasize the beauty. The Bedouin are more interested in racing, while the Europeans are concerned with various show events.

There are between ten thousand and fifteen thousand horses in Jordan. The climate is ideal for raising them. During the summer months, there are five races every Sunday in Amman. Three of the races are reserved for the Bedouin horse breeders.

One of the largest private collections belongs to the uncle of King Hussein, Sherif Nasser bin Jamil. He trains his horses in the Bedouin manner. At six months the colts are put together in a small paddock where they begin to develop their shoulder muscles. Then four or five months later, they are placed in larger

Arabian horses are trained for racing.

rectangular paddocks with gazelles. Gazelles are known for their speed, and they race each other in the morning and evening when it is cool. The colts are challenged by the behavior of the gazelles and join the sport, thereby developing their quarters and hocks. The muscles of the horses are in good shape when the steeds are saddled at eighteen to twenty months.

Mountain horses differ from desert horses. In the mountains, open nostrils and small hoofs are of value, while in the deserts, smaller nostrils and larger hoofs are better adaptations to conditions. Speed and strength are the most admired qualities.

Sherif Nasser can boast of a stable with mares with great bloodlines of horses handed down through his family like heirlooms. He works to improve his horses, to encourage new owners and breeders, and to train new jockeys. King Hussein also has a stable and a riding school where members of his family learn the skills of show riding.

With the climate so well suited to raising horses and a people who appreciate the value of the animals, Jordan can be expected to play an even more important role in this field.

A characteristic feature of Nabataean architecture is the decoration that looks like a staircase at the top of a building.

Chapter 2

ARCHAEOLOGICAL AND HISTORICAL TREASURE HOUSES

Because of Jordan's location in an area of major ancient civilizations, this nation has been the site of many important discoveries by archaeologists. An understanding of the history of this territory is very important to students of the Bible. Jordan has been inhabited by humans for a very long time.

EARLIEST HISTORY

Hunters must have wandered the Jordanian desert longer than 100,000 years ago. They left behind flint tools. In those days, grasslands may have covered the region. The hunters were after elephant, deer, and horse—animals that would have been common where grass was plentiful. A campsite dating to around

Like a puzzle, a workman pieces together bits of broken pottery found in a tomb.

17,500 B.C. has been discovered near the city of Pella. It must have been used by people who hunted and gathered food. Stone tools to butcher and eat animals such as gazelle, sheep, quail, and tortoise have been found nearby.

In that same area, by 10,000 B.C., more organized settlements with dwellings indicate a greater population in the area. The structures were built of stone in a crescent shape. Decorations on the tools indicate the beginnings of art. Some stones with markings may represent an early attempt at counting. Also bone beads, shells, stone vessels, and lumps of red and yellow ocher show the development of crafts. Perhaps most unusual are three large pieces of rock art with carvings on mudstone slabs of concentric squares.

Recently, a human skull almost nine thousand years old has been discovered. It had been covered with plaster that had been

An ancient pottery bowl found in Petra

molded to form features of the face. Here is evidence of reverence for the dead and ceremony in handling the body.

Just across the border on the West Bank of the Jordan River, archaeologists have excavated in the ancient city of Jericho. The earliest levels contain round houses; then, plastered rectangular houses were built. However, the people who lived in them did not have pottery yet. Great defensive walls have been dated to about 7000 B.C. The next levels of occupation here have the remains of pottery.

By around 4000 to 3600 B.C., during the Chalcolithic Period with its use of copper and stone, several settlements in the Jordanian area were active. Down near Aqaba, a team of archaeologists has discovered the remains of a small copper-smelting settlement dating to about 3500 B.C. Houses, storage pits, and brick furnaces have been found along with shell beads, bracelets, and tools of stone, bone, and copper. The copper may have been mined in centers to the north in Wadi Araba. Smaller lumps of the copper may then have been brought to this settlement to be manufactured into useful objects.

Up at Pella, a small settlement of this period consisted of single-room stone houses built on a platform carved out of bedrock. Walls of unshaped limestone were topped by mud bricks reinforced with a plasterlike cement. Storage pits, probably for food, were carved into the floor. The people of this settlement ate barley, wheat, peas, chick-peas, lentils, olives, and the meat from gazelles, cows, goats, pigs, sheep, and large animals—possibly lions. The archaeologists have discovered here stone tools, pierced limestone discs, stone bowls, grinding stones, handmade pottery including fine ware bowls and cups, ceramic spindle whorls (for spinning fabric), and fragments of a ceramic churn for making butter.

Through the Early Bronze Age (about 3000-2100 B.C.), civilization appeared to develop at small settlements. At the end of this period nomads invaded the territory, destroying the main settlements. Peace was not fully restored until the Egyptians dominated the area after 1590 B.C.

INTO WRITTEN RECORDS

The Bible gives us a glimpse into what life must have been like for the nomads who came into this territory. Family groups that passed through the area had to either fight or negotiate their way. Sometimes it was necessary to go around the settled kingdoms if passage was denied. Good flocks and crops were essential to prevent periods of starvation.

*An obelisk dedicated to Queen Hatshepsut is
in the ruins of the temple of Karnak, in Egypt.*

The Hyksos (the shepherd kings) pushed their way into Egypt
from the north around the seventeenth century B.C. With their
horse-drawn chariots, they conquered lands that did not have this
innovation. Certainly parts of the Jordanian area would have been
under their control.

The Hyksos were finally pushed out of Egypt in 1550 B.C.
Within a century the Egyptian Queen Hatshepsut had the area of
Palestine and southern Syria under her control.

Another Egyptian ruler, King Tuthmosis III had representations
of the city Pella carved into the great temple at Karnak as an
indication of the territory over which he had dominion. Pella's
king wrote to the Pharaoh Akhenaten in letters that have been
uncovered in Amarna in Egypt. The communication indicates that
Pella was a caravan stop on the route between Egypt and the
East. A thirteenth-century B.C. Egyptian text states that Pella was a
source of wood that was used in the manufacture of chariot wheel
spokes.

*David being anointed king (above),
and Solomon the Wise (right)*

The Bible also records the story of David who killed over ten thousand people around 1000 B.C. His military conquests led to a kingdom based in Jerusalem. When David fell in love with Bathsheba, the wife of Uriah the Hittite, it was to a battle that he sent Uriah to be killed in order that he might marry Bathsheba. David had created his kingdom when the Egyptians to the south and Assyrians to the north were comparatively weak. His son, Solomon, known for his wisdom, consolidated this power and built both buildings and administrative organization. Solomon entered into marriages to consolidate his diplomatic ties with other powers in the territory. One of the daughters of an Egyptian pharaoh was said to have brought the city of Gezer as a dowry. Ports at the Gulf of Aqaba gave Solomon a base for trading by sea. Archaeologists have found ruins of great public buildings, fine ceramics, and small precious items from this period. The change from tribal warriors to empire had occurred in the space of a few generations.

After Solomon, the kingdom split into two: Israel in the north and Judah in the south. The fight between Omri and his son Ahab, kings of Israel, with the kingdom of Moab may find confirmation in a stone pillar, the Mesha Stele, erected by Mesha, king of Moab, in the ninth century B.C. Written in Moabite, the inscription acknowledges that Omri had oppressed the Moabites for some time, but gives thanks to the god of the Moabites for delivering them from the rule of Israel. The stone is now in the Louvre Museum in Paris.

ATTACKS BY EGYPT, ASSYRIA, BABYLON, AND PERSIA

As neighboring empires gained strength, the Jordanian territory became a pawn in the game of power politics. The gold of the temple and palace of Solomon is reported in the Bible as being carried off by Shishak, king of Egypt. It is thought that this Shishak refers to Shoshenq I, who died shortly after this invasion and whose successor recorded giving at least 383 tons (348,182 kilograms) of precious metals to the gods and goddesses of the cities of Upper and Lower Egypt.

Hostilities and actual warfare continued between the kingdoms in the area. Israel and Judah lost control of many of their regions. However, the next major invasion came from the north—from Assyria. The battle-hardened Assyrians moved south from what is now northern Iraq to extend the power of their empire.

A black obelisk, a pillar with a pointed top, has carvings showing the king of Israel kneeling before the king of Assyria, while Israeli servants present tribute gifts to the Assyrian ruler.

The Jordan River meanders through the desert today just as it has for centuries.

The obelisk is now housed in the British Museum. The Israeli surrender of some of their lands is dated in Assyrian records as 841 B.C.

During the reign of a later king of Israel, Jeroboam II, Israel conquered Damascus in what is now Syria as well as the east bank of the Jordan River down to the Dead Sea. This success was not to last long. Under later kings, Israel found it necessary to call on the Assyrians for help against their enemies. Then another king shifted policy and joined an anti-Assyrian alliance. The Assyrians did not like this, and Damascus and Israel were conquered. The territory was turned into Assyrian provinces governed by Assyrian administrators. The year was 732 B.C.

To the south, the kingdom of Judah came under Assyrian attack on several campaigns. In Jerusalem a tunnel was built to safeguard access to fresh water if the city came under siege. An inscription that documents the completion of this tunnel was

Hezekiah (left) sent tribute to Sennacherib, but the tribute did not satisfy him. Sennacherib (right) conquered Lachish and sat on the throne.

carved into the rock and can be seen today in a museum. Hezekiah, the king of Judah, sent tribute to Sennacherib, ruler of the Assyrians. However, the tribute did not satisfy Sennacherib who proceeded to conquer the nearby city of Lachish. Wonderful stone reliefs of this conquest were carved on the Assyrian palace walls at Nineveh. These carvings give a picture-by-picture description of how the city was taken. They are now preserved in the British Museum. The Assyrians also laid siege to Jerusalem but withdrew suddenly, whether from a plague that hit the soldiers or from demands in the empire is not known.

The Assyrians are the first ones to make reference to the Nabataeans to the south of Edom. The Nabataeans were later to come to power and challenge other empires. The Assyrians lost their empire by 612 B.C. as other powers came to dominate. With the Assyrian presence no longer a restraint, other empires from the East continued to raid Judah until Judah was conquered by the Babylonians in 587 B.C.

Alexander the Great

The Babylonians were conquered by the Persians, who were conquered by the Greeks. Not much is known about what happened in Jordan when the Babylonians and the Persians were the ruling powers. The Persians allowed the Jewish captives to return to Jerusalem. The Nabataeans extended their control into Edom and forced some of the Edomites into Palestine.

GREEK INFLUENCE

Under Alexander the Great the Greeks attacked cities along the Mediterranean coast that could harbor the Persian fleet. After Alexander's death, his empire was carved up among several of his generals. At first the territory of present-day Jordan fell to the lot claimed by Ptolemy I, who took the title of king of Egypt. However, this claim was opposed by Selecus. For generations the Ptolemies and the Seleucids fought over the territory until the Seleucids finally won in 198 B.C.

Under the Greek rule of the Seleucids and the Ptolemies, the territory was prosperous. New buildings were constructed. New cities were founded. Trade was brisk and brought new money into the area. To the south the Nabataeans extended their kingdom to the north and controlled caravan trade with Arabia and Syria. During a period of Seleucid weakness, the Jewish Maccabees seized power in Jerusalem. Later, during a period of conflict in Jerusalem a group of some of these Jews fled to the area around the west bank of the Dead Sea, and wrote the scrolls—leather or papyrus manuscripts—that were found in caves in the twentieth century. These ancient scrolls are important literary and historical finds. They contain information that is being studied by scholars of the Bible and archaeologists. The scrolls also detail how this Jewish community lived two thousand years ago.

THE ROMANS, THE NABATAEANS, AND THE DECAPOLIS

Rome was invited into the territory when some of the Seleucid heirs quarreled over the right to power. The Roman general, Pompey, marched in and took Damascus in 64 B.C. and Jerusalem in 63 B.C. Nabataea in the south was conquered at this time, but the Romans seemed to have maintained this kingdom as a buffer state against the Arabian desert tribes. The Nabataeans dominated the important spice trade. They had learned how to line their cisterns with a plaster that would hold the rainwater for a year or more. They developed a military system of protection for their caravans. They bred camels, sheep, and goats. At the major caravan stops, burial grounds for their people who died along the route were established with large funerary monuments. At first these people lived only in tents. Stone houses were constructed at

The huge entrance to the monastery at Petra dwarfs a person standing in the doorway.

a later date. The famous city of Petra, which they built, appears to have been a religious center for sacrifices and a place for burial of important leaders, as well as a center for trade and learning. Ongoing excavations indicate a possible population of about 30,000. Nabataea became a part of the Roman Empire in A.D. 106 under the Emperor Trajan.

In addition to conquering Damascus and Jerusalem, Pompey established the Decapolis. Largely Greek in language and culture, these northern cities formed a military alliance for protection against the Nabataeans, the Jews, and the desert tribes. The group was never a closed, fixed number; although there were probably ten original allies, other cities joined and withdrew from time to time.

About 43 B.C. Mark Antony became the emperor of the eastern part of the Roman Empire. He shared the empire with Octavius Caesar and Lepidus, forming a ruling body called the *Triumvirate*,

Mark Antony

Cleopatra

"Group of Three." However Antony wanted sole control of Rome so he asked for military and financial aid from Cleopatra, the Ptolemaic queen of Egypt. In return Antony gave Cleopatra Judea and the coastal strip of Arabia down to the Red Sea, as well as parts of Phoenicia and Syria.

Antony and Cleopatra became lovers and later, when Antony was defeated by Octavius in 30 B.C., Cleopatra joined Antony in death by suicide. Their story has been dramatized in many famous works of literature, particularly in John Dryden's play *All for Love* (1677) and William Shakespeare's play *Antony and Cleopatra* (1607).

CHRISTIANITY, CHALLENGES TO ROME, THE BYZANTINE EMPIRE

The New Testament accounts of the life of Jesus tell of his baptism by John in the Jordan River. John was later taken

Roman Emperor Trajan (left) and Arab Queen Zenobia

prisoner and beheaded. The traditional site for this event and the dance of Salome at the palace of Herod is Machaerus to the east of the Dead Sea. Journeys and healings by Jesus are reported east of the Jordan River. The apostle Paul's journey to Damascus from Jerusalem may have taken him over the East Bank route. Later, other apostles of the Christian religion must have come into the region to begin the challenge to the pagan gods and goddesses. Early church foundations have been uncovered in the region.

Revolts against Roman power in Galilee and Judea led to the fall of Jerusalem in A.D. 70 and Roman consolidation of power in the region. Nabataea was annexed in A.D. 106 by the Roman Emperor Trajan. Towns and cities in what is now Jordan prospered under Roman rule. The whole territory, except the Decapolis, was made part of the new Roman province called Arabia Petraea.

Rome still had its challengers. In the third century A.D., Zenobia, the Arabic queen of the city of Palmyra in what is now Syria, carved out a little empire for herself. While Rome was being

Constantine the Great brought Christianity to the area.

pressed in northern Italy by barbarians, Zenobia attacked Egypt, annexed most of Syria, and then took Bithnynia on the Bosporus in Asia Minor. Known as the Queen of the East, by A.D. 270 she had an empire that controlled trade routes important to Rome and maintained a court known for intellectual brilliance. An Arab, she borrowed regal customs from both Eastern and Western empires. Zenobia went into battle with her cavalry. When the Romans were able to turn their attention to this threat, they were able to defeat the Palmyreans. Zenobia fled on a female camel, swifter than a horse, to avoid capture. She almost made it across the Euphrates River to safety. However, the Romans captured her and, according to one version of the story, took her back to Rome. Another source claims she committed suicide.

Under the Roman emperor Constantine, Christianity became the recognized religion of the empire in A.D. 313. This emperor renamed the ancient city of Byzantium after himself— Constantinople (now named Istanbul in Turkey). It became the capital of the Byzantine Empire that took over the eastern parts of

The Persians invaded Jerash in 614 and in 636 the city was conquered by the Muslims.

the Roman Empire. East of the Jordan River about twenty churches were important enough to have bishops, many of whom attended important church conferences to decide doctrine. New religious buildings were erected, and pilgrimages were encouraged to places holy to the Christian religion. Jerash became a pilgrimage center.

Several peaceful centuries were interrupted in the sixth and seventh centuries by warfare between the Byzantine Empire and the Sassanian Persian Empire to the east. In 614 the Persians captured Damascus and Jerusalem. In Jerash, two goalposts in the sports arena are reminders of the Persian love for the game of polo. Also, an unfinished palace at Mashitta, built by the Persian king as a winter home, is a fine example of Persian architectural decorations. While the Emperor Heraclius was able to restore Byzantine rule by 627, the empire was weakened by the fighting. It was unable to withstand the attack in 636 that brought the area that was to be Jordan under Muslim rule.

Chapter 3

ISLAMIC TERRITORY

The territory of Jordan was among the first to feel the impact of the new religion of Islam that swept out of Arabia and quickly challenged countries in Africa, Europe, and Asia. This land was involved in the wars that the Christian crusaders brought to the area. It became a battleground in World War I. The location of Jordan between contending world forces often has focused the spotlight of history on this land.

SWORD OF ISLAM

Muhammad, the prophet of Islam, who lived in Mecca and Medina in Arabia from about A.D. 570 to 632, proclaimed a message that inspired the Arab tribes to take this new religion to unbelievers or infidels. Within a century the Muslims had conquered lands that stretched from the Atlantic Ocean on the west to the Indus River on the east.

The first battle between forces of the Byzantine Empire and the
Muslims took place in 629 at Muta, south of Kerak, on what is
now Jordanian territory. A small Muslim force was defeated by
the Byzantines and three of their leaders (Zaid bin Harith, Jaafer
bin Abu Talib, and Abdallah bin Ruaha) were killed. The three are
buried at a mosque in Mazar. The Arabs retreated to Medina to
regroup. Their new military leader, Khalid bin Walid, proved to
be a genius at strategy. The next year Muhammad led a force
against the oasis of Tabuk. There an agreement was reached with
some neighboring settlements granting people the right to retain
their property and religion in return for the payment of annual
tribute. When Muhammad died there was a split between Muslims
as to who should succeed him. Eventually Abu Bakr became the
next ruler.

The only places that Islam reached outside of the Arabian Peninsula
during the lifetime of Muhammad were in what is now Jordan.

In 633, the Arabs invaded Jordan and Syria. They won the first
battle and overran much of the territory except for a few cities like
Jerusalem and Caesarea. But the decisive battle against the Byzantine
forces numbering fifty thousand came in 636 at Yarmouk to the
north, and the Muslims took over the territory.

The rulers of the Islamic forces were called *caliphs*. When Caliph
Abu Bakr died, he was succeeded by Umar bin Khattab, a man
who had helped conquer Galilee, the Jordan lowlands, and central
and southern Palestine. Muawiayah of the Umayyad Dynasty
became caliph in the seventh century and moved the seat of
administrative power from Mecca to Damascus where it remained
until another line, the Abbasids, moved it to Baghdad in the
middle of the eighth century.

While Damascus was the center of the Islamic world (661-750),

Jordan had an important role. The Arabs retained their love of the desert and built beautiful hunting lodges and palaces in the Jordanian desert. Frescoes in one of these show the caliph with his conquered royalty: the kings of Byzantium, the Visigoths of Spain, and rulers of Persia and Ethiopia. The pilgrimage to Mecca became important during this period, and the route from Damascus followed along the old road on the East Bank to Ma'an where it turned off toward Mecca. Trade caravans developed along this route, and both pilgrims and merchants were forced to pay protection money to tribes in control of the territory.

The dynasty of the Umayyad leaders was followed by the Abbasids, a family that originated in the village of Humaima between Ma'an and Aqaba. The Abbasids moved the capital to Baghdad, now in Iraq, around 750. Jordan fell into decline, no longer providing homes for the rulers or maintaining the main pilgrimage road. As the power of the Abbasids declined, their empire began breaking apart. The Fatimids took over power in Egypt and pressed on into the East Bank while the Seljuk Turks from the north moved into the area. By 1071, the Turks had ousted the Fatimids, but the Bedouin Arabs were really the ones in control of localities.

CRUSADERS, SALADIN, AND THE MAMLUKS

The Western Crusaders marched into the territory next. These European princes and their followers were motivated by a religious zeal to capture the Christian holy places from the Muslims, by a love of adventure, and in some cases by the hope of younger sons for new land to rule. The Crusaders took Jerusalem in 1099. Jordanian land was parceled out to the victorious knights

*In 1099 the Crusaders captured the city of Jerusalem
(left), but in 1187 Saladin (right) reclaimed the city.*

who proceeded to build castles to defend their territory. The ruins
of some of these remain to this day. The most famous at Kerak
was on the old highway and had been a chief city of Moab.

A great Muslim general rose to challenge the Crusaders. His
name was Salah al-Din or, as he was known in the West, Saladin.
The story is told that the Christian nobles were celebrating a very
important wedding at the castle at Kerak when Saladin arrived to
attack the fortress. When the lady of the castle sent banquet dishes
out to Saladin, Saladin gallantly inquired where the newlywed
couple would be staying so that he could avoid bombarding that
section. When a bonfire message from the castle brought
reinforcements, Saladin had to withdraw. Later, however, Saladin
retook the land from the Crusaders, and in 1187 conquered
Jerusalem, a city also holy to the Muslims. While the Crusaders
left the Arabs with suspicions and hostility toward Europeans, the

Europeans carried home with them new customs, food, clothing, and learning that they had gained from their contact with the civilizations of the East.

Saladin began the Ayyubid Dynasty that lasted until 1250 when the Mamluks came to power in Egypt. The word *mamluk* means "slave." Under the Mamluks, succession of power passed to a military leader, to an ex-slave who had achieved power, or to a member of the elite bodyguard. They rebuilt some of the fortresses and fought off an invasion by the Mongolians at the Battle of Ain Jalut in 1260. However, the territory did not prosper under the Mamluks. A plague and heavy taxation took their toll. Attacks by the Bedouin showed the weakened power. Desert nomads captured Kerak and even went on to Jerusalem.

THE OTTOMAN EMPIRE

After the defeat of the Mamluks in 1517, the land passed to the control of the Ottoman Turks for a period of four hundred years. It was not a bright period. Under Suleyman the Magnificent, the pilgrimage road from Damascus to Medina and Mecca was reestablished, but farther west of its former location. Almost at the desert, this road was the cause of some new forts being built. However, the Turks were not able to staff all the forts, and so the Turkish officials subsidized some of the Bedouin tribes in the area by bribing them with gold as the pilgrim caravans passed through the territory. Although the land was theoretically under Turkish control, the real authority lay with the Bedouin and some leading families in the few remaining towns. Feuds between the tribes did not provide much peace.

Because of his campaigns in Egypt (above),
Napoleon (right) focused European attention on the Near East.

At the beginning of the nineteenth century, Napoleon's
campaigns in Egypt focused European attention again on the Near
East. European travelers visited the area and wrote adventure
stories about their trips. The Swiss explorer Johann Ludwig
Burckhardt discovered the archaeological site of Petra.

During the nineteenth century, the Turks had a refugee problem
because of a war with Russia. They settled Circassian, Caucasian,
and other refugees (all non-Arab people from the north) in the
area with grants of land and aid in establishing towns. Even the
refugees who were Muslim were not Arabs and did not speak
Arabic. The Bedouin did not take kindly to having newcomers
settle on their land. The refugees considered the Bedouin
barbarians who should be sent back to the desert. The Turks
hoped to gain control by playing one group against the other.

One group of Christians settled at Madaba around the ruins of an old church building. In 1884 a monk of the Greek Orthodox faith wrote to his superior about a mosaic pavement there that contained the names of the important cities of earlier times. This find turned out to be a pictorial map that dates to around the sixth century and is a great treasure. Unfortunately, the architect assigned to build a church there did not think the map worth much and put a column on it, damaging the mosaic. In 1896 a librarian for the head of the Greek Orthodox church assessed the real value of the map.

Toward the end of the nineteenth century, the Turks tightened their control of the area by establishing military and police garrisons. Still, lawlessness often prevailed. The Turks built a telegraph line from Damascus to Medina and Mecca and in 1900 started work on a railroad that was to be used exclusively for religious purposes for pilgrims to the Islamic holy cities. By 1908 the section from Amman to Medina was completed.

Kerak was the site of an uprising against the Turks when the governors attempted to take a census of the people in 1910. The revolt was put down, and the leaders who failed were thrown over the sides of the castle to die on the rocks below. At the end of Turkish rule, there were more towns and more areas under cultivation. While the government had greater control of some areas, especially in the south, the Bedouin tribes often had the law in their own hands.

THE HASHEMITE FAMILY, WORLD WAR I, LAWRENCE OF ARABIA

When the Turks proposed the building of the railroad route to Mecca, one person who doubted their motivation was Sherif

Sherif Hussein (left) and T.E. Lawrence (right)

Hussein, the great-grandfather of the present king. Hussein was head of the Hashemite family. He was a direct descendant of Muhammad and the guardian of the Islamic holy city of Mecca. He suspected that the Turks were more interested in being able to move their troops into the Arabian Peninsula.

Sherif Hussein had lived in Constantinople for fifteen years at the Turkish sultan's request, to keep him from challenging Turkish power. Hussein's four sons had been educated in the Turkish capital. He knew the political ambitions of Turkey, so he asked the British government to help the Arabs to gain independence from Turkey. At first the British were not enthusiastic about the suggestion, but by the time that Turkey had sided with Germany in World War I, the British gave support. The Arabs revolted in June 1916. Hussein and his four sons were supplied with guns by the British. One of the British agents who worked with the Arabs was T. E. (Thomas Edward) Lawrence,

Turkish troops in Damascus were defeated by the Arabs and British.

whose exploits won him public attention and the name, "Lawrence of Arabia." One of Hussein's sons, Emir Faisal, took charge of the military campaign and worked with Lawrence. They captured Aqaba. Their raids on the Turkish railroad disrupted troop movements and supply shipments. The British army was moving north in a parallel action to the west. As the Arabs moved south, larger numbers of fighters joined their cause. The Arab and British forces met at Damascus in October 1918 and defeated the Turks.

With Turkey on the losing side in World War I, the Ottoman Empire's control of the region ended. Great Britain, France, Russia, and Italy had entered into a secret treaty in 1915, planning an independent Muslim power to be set up in Arabia. However, the French wanted to protect their interests in Lebanon and Syria, and divided with Britain spheres of influence over the countries of the Near East. The British minister for foreign affairs, Arthur

*In 1919 Prince Faisal (center foreground) and Lawrence of Arabia
(second row, second from right) attended the Peace Conference in Paris.*

Balfour, also gave support to the establishment of a national home for the Jewish people in Palestine, so long as nothing would be done to change the rights of existing non-Jewish people there.

Hussein's son, Faisal, was greeted in Damascus as a conquering hero. He was selected at the meeting of the Arab Congress in March 1920 to be king of all Syria, Lebanon, Transjordan (the territory on the East Bank), and Palestine. However, the world powers set up mandates from the League of Nations. France was to be in charge of Syria and Lebanon, and Great Britain was to supervise the rest of the territory. When the French refused to recognize Faisal as ruler in Syria, the British made room for him on a throne in the country of Iraq.

Another of the sons of Hussein, the Emir Abdullah, arrived in Ma'an in January 1921 with an army of two hundred with the intention of driving the French out of Syria. The British agents at

Winston Churchill (left) of Great Britain and two of Hussein's sons, King Faisal (left) and King Abdullah (right)

Kerak allowed Abdullah to establish a government at Amman. Winston Churchill, secretary of the colonial office, and other British officials met with Abdullah who agreed to stop his action against the French, to renounce rights to Iraq, to maintain order in Transjordan, and to recognize the British mandate. In return Abdullah received subsidies and the promise of the future recognition of the independence of Transjordan. On May 25, 1923 Abdullah formally proclaimed Transjordan an autonomous state under the League of Nations mandate. In return for financial subsidies, Great Britain controlled foreign policy and oversaw Transjordan's finances.

TRANSJORDAN

The territory to be governed presented a number of problems. Order had to be restored. Settled communities objected to paying high taxes while the Bedouin were free of them. The tribes looked to their leaders as the judges of disputes. The tribes had a tradition of raids on each other even across the national boundaries. Abdullah asked a British officer, Frederick G. Peake, who had experience with the Egyptian Camel Corps to form a peacekeeping desert patrol for Transjordan. Peake had fought from Aqaba to Damascus in World War I, so he knew the territory. His force was called the Arab Legion.

Serious problems developed from raids into Transjordan by Bin Saud and his tribe, the Wahhabis, who were enemies of the Hashemites. Hussein, the father of Abdullah, was in control of the holy cities of Mecca and Medina in Arabia. After the Turkish legislature abolished the caliphate, the Islamic authority, Hussein laid claim to it by virtue of his descent from Muhammad and his office as guardian of the holy cities. Opposition from other Islamic countries was intense.

When the British realized that Hussein would not be able to command the loyalty of the other Muslims, they negotiated with Bin Saud and asked him not to attack Hussein. But Bin Saud moved in to occupy in 1924. Hussein escaped and eventually set up residence in Cyprus because his presence might have endangered the kingdoms of his sons in Transjordan and Iraq. In 1933 a treaty was signed by Transjordan and Saudi Arabia stopping raids on the southern border.

In 1930, John Bagot Glubb, a British officer with experience in Iraq, was asked to organize a desert mobile force, known as the Desert Patrol, as part of the Arab Legion. Glubb spoke Arabic well and had an appreciation for the desert Arabs. He built up his force with carefully selected men from important tribes. This force was given intensive training including the skills of reading and writing. Soon this group had a waiting list for the opportunity to

Mounted soldiers of the Arab Legion

enlist. Members took great pride in their unit. Their task involved patrolling 750 miles (1,207 kilometers) of borders and stopping tribal raiding from the north of Arabia.

Abdullah worked with the British to put laws in place that would assist with the process of governing. A Legislative Council was elected in 1929. Its function was to develop laws that the *emir* (the title for the ruler) would pass or veto. The emir could still rule by decree and the British resident authority could overrule the decisions. In 1939 the power of the British resident was diminished, and Abdullah reconstituted the legislative council into a Council of Ministers.

Ownership and registration of land by individuals helped to settle many of the nomads into new styles of living involving some cultivation. More schools were established. Although there were revolts and intrigues against Abdullah, he had established more stability in his country and had made more progress by 1931. Further consolidation took place during the second decade of his rule. While Abdullah was interested in economic development, the world economy and the mandate status of the country often made growth difficult to achieve. Attempts were made to enlarge areas under cultivation through artificial irrigation. It was recognized that it was not only impossible but also unprofitable to convert the nomads into cultivators. While most Bedouin had some land in grain, they needed to rely on livestock breeding, at which they were expert. Education, health services, and transportation improved during this period.

World War II was not fought on Transjordan territory, but the conflict had its effect on the country. The Arab Legion under Glubb provided assistance to a British force that seized Habbaniya and Baghdad in Iraq to keep the Germans out. After France fell to Germany, the German-backed Vichy French took control of Syria and Lebanon. The Arab Legion participated briefly in that sector. The Legion also guarded supply lines, pipelines, transportation targets, and British installations in Egypt. It was the only Arab force that gave active support to the Allies.

The political benefits to the country were great. In order to win the loyalty of the Arabs to the Allied cause, in 1941 Great Britain allowed Abdullah to act without obtaining British consent. As a reward to the Transjordanians for their support, the British granted full independence to the country on March 22, 1946.

THE HASHEMITE KINGDOM OF TRANSJORDAN

Although Abdullah was enthroned as king with due ceremony on May 25, 1946, the country was still dependent on Great Britain for money and for the training of the Arab Legion. Other Arab countries reacted negatively to the British interests safeguarded in the treaty between Transjordan and Great Britain. When Transjordan applied for membership in the United Nations in 1946, countries raised questions about whether Transjordan was fully independent or still under British control. The Soviet Union vetoed the application for several years. It was 1955 before Jordan gained admission to the United Nations.

Transjordan was active in international politics nevertheless. In 1947 Abdullah negotiated treaties with Turkey and Iraq. Britain renegotiated its treaty with Transjordan to clarify the independence of the latter. In 1948 Britain still had certain peacetime military advantages in return for economic and social aid. As early as 1943 and 1944, Transjordan had been involved in the discussions preliminary to the formation of the Arab League and became one of the original members in 1945. Egypt, Iraq, Transjordan, Lebanon, Saudi Arabia, Syria, and Yemen made up the Arab League. Abdullah hoped for the formation of a "Greater Syria." He felt that Arab unity would be furthered by the joining of Transjordan, Syria, and Palestine into one country to be followed later by the inclusion of Iraq. This idea was opposed by Syrian nationalists, the leaders of Egypt and Saudi Arabia (who did not want to back the Hashemites), the French, and the Zionists (who wanted a Jewish state in Israel).

In May 1948 British troops moved out of Palestine, and Israel proclaimed its independence. Arab armies moved into the territory. The Transjordan Arab Legion was able to hold the West Bank, including the important old city of Jerusalem. In December Abdullah was proclaimed king of all Palestine. In April 1949 the country's name was changed to the Hashemite Kingdom of Jordan

In 1948 British troops moved out of Palestine (left) and David Ben Gurion (right) signed a document proclaiming the new state of Israel.

and three Palestinians, West Bank Arabs, were included in the Cabinet. Armistices were signed by most Arab countries.

Gaza to the south on the Mediterranean was in Arab hands and declared itself an independent state. However in a 1949 meeting at Jericho, Arab leaders and delegates from refugee camps voted for union with Jordan. By action of the Cabinet and legislature on April 24, 1950, the West Bank was annexed. Gaza was placed under United Nations protection. Some of the members of the Arab League were hostile to these actions by Jordan.

Annexation brought many problems. The Palestinians tended to have more education and business skills. They had their own loyalties that did not include a close association with the royal family. The refugees that were displaced by the Israelis in the territory that became Israel had a difficult time. Some 400,000 people had to live in refugee camps because the Jordanian economy could not support them. About 400,000 other Arabs were still in homes in the West Bank. The refugees who had

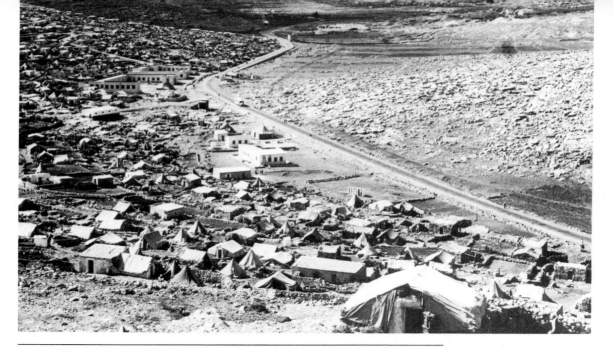

Living conditions in the camps, such as Dhesheh Camp in Bethlehem, with temporary housing and food and health problems, were not good.

money found that their accounts in Israeli banks had been frozen so they had no access to them. The United Nations Relief and Works Agency, along with private voluntary agencies, began aid to the refugees. The Jordanians often resented the refugees who caused burdens on their limited water and food supplies. Only 6 percent of the land of Jordan was west of the river, but two-thirds of the population were now Palestinian.

A year of political unrest followed in 1951. Three-fourths of the wheat and barley crop were ruined by drought. Inflation caused rising prices. Other Arab countries were accusing Abdullah of being a British puppet and soft on the Zionists in order to increase his territory by winning the West Bank. There were threats on Abdullah's life. On Friday, July 20, 1951, as King Abdullah was in Jerusalem on his way to attend religious services at the al-Aqsa Mosque, he was assassinated. The gunman also took a shot at the king's grandson, Hussein, but the bullet was deflected by a medal on his uniform.

Chapter 4

KING HUSSEIN'S REIGN

The grandson who was present at King Abdullah's assassination was soon to become king of Jordan—King Hussein I bin Talal. He has survived many attempts on his life.

BEFORE THE THRONE

Hussein's father, King Talal, had been sent to England for his college education. He attended the Royal Military College at Sandhurst. Talal married his mother's niece, Sharifa Zein, who had lived in the sophisticated city of Cairo. Hussein was born on November 14, 1935. Later, Zein bore two more sons, Muhammad and Hassan, and a daughter, Basma.

Hussein grew up in modest circumstances. His father, Talal, insisted that he have a good grounding in Arabic. His grandfather, Abdullah, was more interested in the boy's religious background. Hussein had a close relationship with his grandfather. From Abdullah, Hussein learned family traditions and the ways of the Bedouin. Abdullah loved to go to his black tent that was pitched at Shuneh beside the Dead Sea. There leaders of various tribes would be entertained with traditional Bedouin hospitality. On the day of his death, Abdullah is reported to have said of Hussein:

Hussein, at age seventeen, in Switzerland with his brother Muhammad

"He is the elite of the elite. He is the continuity of my dynasty." It was his grandfather who insisted that Hussein wear his uniform that day—a fortunate choice since the assassin's bullet was deflected by a medal.

Abdullah's assassination happened when Hussein was fifteen years old. His father was out of the country receiving medical treatment. Talal's half brother, Naif, stepped in as regent and was plotting to be named king. Hussein's mother fought to have Abdullah's funeral postponed until Talal could return. Although there was concern about Talal's fitness because of a condition of mental illness, the government backed Talal and moved two Bedouin regiments to Amman. Naif got the message and left the country for the rest of his life.

Now a crown prince, Hussein was sent to the prestigious Harrow School in England. Hussein's cousin, Faisal, the heir to the throne of Iraq, was also at that school and the two became

At Harrow School in England, Crown Prince Hussein of Jordan (right) shakes hands with Prince Mukarram Jah of India.

good friends. The headmaster at the school found Hussein to be determined—even headstrong—but one who would thrive on difficulties and be a strong ruler.

During King Talal's reign, a new constitution was approved in January 1952 reducing the king's powers and making the Cabinet responsible to Parliament. Some on the East Bank were doubtful about the value of this change because of the representation of the West Bank in the Parliament. Also Talal seemed to be changing his father's foreign policy by leaning toward Syria and Egypt. Jordan joined the Arab League's Collective Security Pact.

King Talal's health began to deteriorate and trips to Europe for medical treatment were necessary. A regency council was established by the Cabinet to exercise the powers of government. Two foreign doctors were asked to examine the king, and they declared that he was unfit to rule. The Parliament asked that the king abdicate in favor of his son, Hussein. Talal agreed to do so. He lived in Turkey until his death in July 1972.

The young King Hussein stands before his throne as he reads the constitutional oath.

Hussein was with his mother and siblings in a hotel in Switzerland in August 1952 when his father abdicated. He was handed an envelope by the hotel page that was addressed to "His Majesty King Hussein." In this way, he was given official notice of his new role. It was just three months before his seventeenth birthday.

EARLY YEARS OF RULE

Hussein assumed constitutional power on May 2, 1953, the same day that his cousin, Faisal, began his rule in Iraq. The nation that Hussein governed was a country divided into factions with East Bank and West Bank interests. Jordan was in the midst of nations in the Near East that were battlegrounds for competing groups. Moreover, the Near East was the target of maneuvering by world powers; the United States, the Soviet Union, Great Britain, and France were all interested in winning influence.

Talal had opened the country to more democratic forces, and

the Communists and Socialists moved in to win support. A series of new prime ministers were appointed. But under Hussein the government shut down the Communist newspaper and took a more conservative line. Hussein opposed communism, with its atheistic policy, as contrary to Islam.

Egypt and Iraq vied for leadership of the Arab countries. Gamal Abdul Nasser had seized power in Egypt from King Farouk in July 1952 in a military coup. With Iraq and other Muslim countries, Turkey formed the Baghdad Pact in 1955. Nasser saw Iraq's leadership role in the pact and tried to undermine it. Instead an Egyptian, Syrian, and Saudi Arabian bloc was formed in competition. Jordan announced in November 1955 that it would not align itself with either group.

The appointment of a prime minister known to be in favor of the Baghdad Pact was followed by riots in Amman and further changes in prime ministers. Jordan swung back to a policy of neutrality between the blocs. Later in 1956, an agreement for military cooperation was reached with Syria, Lebanon, and Egypt, and in July an economic union with Syria was announced.

In March 1956 Hussein announced the dismissal of Glubb as commander-in-chief of the Jordanian Armed Forces and his replacement by Major General Radi 'Annab. Friction had been building between the king and Glubb over a variety of matters. The dismissal of Glubb aroused an outcry in Great Britain where he was viewed as a hero. While British officers were retained in a training capacity and the British continued their financial support of the armed forces, many Jordanians felt happier with Arab officers in command. The Arabs were wary of Great Britain because of the role it played in the creation of Israel.

Tension along the borders with Israel continued to be great. The

Left: King Hussein in 1953 with his brothers Muhammad (left) and Hassan (right).
Right: General John Glubb, former commander of the Arab Legion

refugees, use of water from the Jordan River, the border definition, and the status of Jerusalem were all matters of friction. When Israel, Great Britain, and France attacked Egypt in 1956 in a dispute over control of the Suez Canal, attitudes hardened. After new elections in Jordan, the 1948 treaty with Great Britain was discarded, and British troops left the country.

Syria had moved over to the Soviet sphere of influence. The United States announced that it was determined to preserve Jordan's independence and shipped arms in an airlift to Amman in September 1957. Jordan requested the withdrawal of Syrian troops that had been serving under a joint command. There was a partial break in diplomatic relations with Egypt.

During 1957 there was an attempt to unseat Hussein. Nasser, the Egyptian ruler, was stirring up some of the army officers to support the idea of an Arab union by getting rid of the king. The Bedouin troops who were intensely loyal to Hussein were ordered to move out into the desert without ammunition—an order that they interpreted as getting them out of the way so they could not defend the king. They refused to obey these orders. The king, himself, had to go to them to show that he was alive. The person suspected of leading the coup was packed off to Egypt. There followed a purge of the army officers who had let politics carry them away from their loyalty to Jordan. The king's courage to stand up to threats of the loss of his kingdom and to the extension of the Communist power base won him public admiration at home and abroad. His limitation of constitutional freedoms at home in order to secure his own power base and defend his country from external attack drew criticism.

On February 1, 1958 Egypt and Syria had signed an agreement to be united in the United Arab Republic based on the principles of Arab nationalism and socialism. On February 14, the merger of the kingdoms of Jordan and Iraq into a union called the Arab Federation was announced by Hussein and King Faisal of Iraq. Both unions had many potential problems because of differing national interests.

In the Arab Federation, the family ties between the leaders made it easy for Hussein to assume the role of deputy to Faisal. The Jordanian Secret Service uncovered a plot inspired by Egypt's Nasser. Army officers were to attempt a coup in Amman and in Baghdad, the capital of Iraq. The information was shared with Iraq, but the officers in charge did not appear to take it seriously and the coup succeeded. Army officers there established a Socialist government and killed members of the royal family.

The situation for Jordan was very hazardous. Oil was being cut off by Iraq, Syria, and Egypt and by the neutral policy adopted by Saudi Arabia. Hussein, with Cabinet support, showed great courage in asking for British and American troop support to save

In 1965 King Hussein (right) named his brother Hassan crown prince.

his country. Being closer, the British flew in paratroopers from Cyprus. Hussein immediately pointed to the involvement of Nasser in the plots. Jordan was given world support and economic aid. At this time the port facilities at Aqaba on the Red Sea became a significant trade outlet.

Plots against the king and Jordanian officials continued. Syrian MIG fighters tried to down the king's plane and would have succeeded except for the pilot's skill at outmaneuvering them. The king's nose drops were laced with acid that would have killed him and a poison plot was uncovered. The prime minister was killed with a time bomb in 1960.

On October 3, 1960, at the age of twenty-four, the king made a speech in the United Nations that was to win Jordan many friends in the international community. At home, the king's courage had demonstrated that he was a worthy successor to his grandfather. In 1965, Hussein named his younger brother, Hassan, the crown prince.

Jordanian tanks mobilize during the Six Day War.

LOSS OF THE WEST BANK

Relationships with Syria and Egypt continued to be strained. Activities of Palestinian groups such as the PLO caused increased difficulties with Israel, and Israeli raids into Jordan brought bitter feelings in return. Syria and the PLO called on Jordanians to revolt against the king.

As tensions increased with Israel, Hussein flew to Egypt and met with Nasser to sign a defense agreement placing Hussein's military under Egyptian command. Jordanian troops went into action along with those of Egypt, Syria, Iraq, and Saudi Arabia in June 1967 in the Six Day War against Israel. The confusion in military intelligence and in joint commands made the situation very frustrating for the king. Although Jordanian troops fought bravely, often with little help from their allies, the Israelis occupied and held all territory west of the Jordan River. It is estimated that between 150,000 and 250,000 people fled from the West Bank to join the existing 650,000 refugee population.

Several changes in government structure, including the formation of a Senate with fifteen representatives from inhabitants of the West Bank and fifteen from eastern Jordan, were made to accommodate the new conditions in the nation. Instability along the borders continued when Israeli commandos blew up part of the system of the main irrigation project, the Ghor Canal. Jordan appealed for United Nations intervention.

The Palestinian fighters were at first honored by the Jordanian people who sympathized with their cause. However, these guerrilla fighters, called *fedayeen*, soon fell to fighting among themselves as well as bringing retaliatory raids on the Jordanians. The fedayeen engaged in open fighting in Amman, making several parts of Jordan unsafe for civilians. There were several assassination attempts on the king and hijackings of planes of Western airlines. The army finally restored order. Syrian forces invaded Jordan but were repelled. The guerrilla forces were ordered out of Jordan, and many went on to fight in Lebanon.

The king continued to search for long-term solutions to the Palestinian problem. In 1972 he proposed a United Arab Kingdom that he would head with a federal capital in Amman and a separate capital in Jerusalem for the Palestinian sector. Each sector would have separate councils. Other nations did not like the plan. There was another attempted coup that was stopped in 1972.

In the Middle East October War of 1973, Jordan sent troops to back up Syria on the Golan Heights. However, it did not open up a front against Israel along its borders with that country. At the Arab Summit Conference at Rabat in October 1974, Hussein reluctantly went along with the resolution that unanimously recognized the PLO as the sole legitimate representative of the Palestinians with the right to establish authority over any

Egyptian President Anwar Sadat, U.S. President Jimmy Carter,
and Israeli Prime Minister Menachem Begin at Camp David

liberated Palestinian territory. Since this action amounted to a release of Jordan's claims on the West Bank, the nation's relationship with the other Arab countries improved.

Although Hussein was perceived as sitting on the fence with respect to Egyptian President Anwar Sadat's efforts to work out a peace settlement with Israel, he opposed Israel's plan to keep the West Bank. Jordan wanted a Palestinian homeland whose people would decide its relationship to Jordan by referendum. Hussein refused to join the Camp David talks between Egypt and Israel. Jordan joined other Arab states in enforcing sanctions against Egypt.

With the outbreak of war between Iraq and Iran, Jordan became a strong supporter of Iraq. This friendship brought hostility with Syria and troop buildups on both sides of that border. Following the Israeli invasion of Lebanon in 1982, President Ronald Reagan of the United States proposed the establishment of an autonomous Palestinian authority on the West Bank that was to be associated with Jordan. While the king claimed to support the idea, the PLO did not, so the plan failed. Jordan did give backing to Yassir Arafat of the PLO when his leadership was challenged by more radical Syrian-backed groups in Lebanon in 1983.

*After establishing diplomatic relations, President Hosni Mubarak
of Egypt visited King Hussein in Amman, Jordan.*

In March 1984, the first elections in seventeen years for the
House of Deputies were held in Jordan. It was the first in which
women were allowed to vote. Since Israel controlled the West
Bank, polling places were located only on the East Bank. West
Bank delegates were elected. The vote showed the opposition to
the Reagan Plan and an increase in support for Muslim
fundamentalist groups. With Jordan critical of United States
policy, Congress in the United States was unwilling to vote
military supplies to Jordan. Jordan then turned to the Soviets and
France for military supplies and help in solving the Palestinian
problem. The United States president offered economic aid, but
the Senate provided that it be spread out over twenty-seven
months instead of fifteen.

In November 1984 Jordan reestablished diplomatic relations
with Egypt and received Egyptian President Hosni Mubarak's
support for a proposal for peace negotiations that called for the

convening of a conference of all concerned parties in the Middle East including the PLO as an equal partner with other nations. Under this plan, Israel was required to accept the principle of giving land for peace, thereby restoring the occupied territories in return for a comprehensive peace treaty with Arab nations.

While the PLO at first agreed to this peace initiative, Arafat's refusal to go along with United Nations Security Council resolutions 242 and 338 ended in the king scrapping the February 1985 Jordanian-PLO accord and ordering the PLO offices in Jordan closed in June of 1986. Finally in July 1988 the king severed legal and administrative ties to the West Bank and relinquished responsibility for the territory, which he said was to be the obligation of the Palestinian leaders. This move shifted the burden for what becomes of the occupied territories to the PLO leaders and permitted Jordan to concentrate on East Bank development. The possibility, however, of a West Bank referendum vote to rejoin Jordan was not eliminated.

Economic conditions in Jordan worsened in 1989. The country needed to renegotiate its foreign debt, and the International Monetary Fund required an economic program that caused great price increases. Riots over the higher prices broke out in Jordan in April. There was dissatisfaction with the mismanagement of the country by the prime minister then in power. The king changed prime ministers and called for new elections. One of the concerns about the results of that ballot was the number of Muslim fundamentalists elected—still a minority but growing in power. The new prime minister pledged to provide more freedom and democracy to Jordanian citizens.

The Iraqi invasion of Kuwait in 1990 resulted in severe hardships for Jordan. Although Jordan took an official position of

King Hussein was not in support of the use of force against Iraq in 1991.

compliance with the United Nations sanctions against Iraq, King Hussein was critical of the Saudi invitation to the United States to protect Saudi Arabian territory. There was great popular support in Jordan for the Iraqi president, Saddam Hussein.

The consequences of the Gulf War for Jordan were a shutdown of income from exports of fruits and vegetables and much of the trade through the Port of Aqaba, the abandonment of tourist business, and the loss of development aid from the West and from the rich Arab states that previously gave support. Jordanians formerly working in other Middle Eastern countries flooded into their homeland along with foreign refugees, resulting in heavy demands for unanticipated social services. Moreover, the currency previously coming from the overseas workers was lost to the economy.

Queen Noor talks to Asian refugees from Kuwait

While unpopular abroad, at home the King's Gulf War efforts were hailed. At the end of 1990, the king and leaders of major political groupings within Jordan reached agreement on a National Charter. Political parties were legalized in return for their recognition of the legitimacy of the Hashemite monarchy. All Jordanians are eligible for public office. In 1994 Israel and Jordan signed a comprehensive peace treaty.

King Hussein has been married four times and has five sons and seven daughters. His first two marriages ended in divorce. His third wife, Queen Alia, was killed in a helicopter crash in 1977. His fourth marriage was to an American of Arab ancestry, Lisa Halaby, known as Queen Noor. In addition to her four children, she made a home for the young children of Queen Alia.

Chapter 5

JORDANIAN SOCIETY

With the stresses and strains in the history and in the present conditions of this country, Jordan is not the easiest nation to govern. The changes that are taking place may well cause new opportunities and new challenges in the basic structures of society such as government, religion, education, and the arts.

GOVERNMENT

The first general election in twenty-two years and sweeping political reforms in 1989 showed movement toward greater democracy. Reforms included the removal of regulations on the press, lifting martial law, and reducing the power of domestic security forces. In 1991 King Hussein canceled nearly all remaining provisions of martial law. These reforms increased freedoms provided by the 1952 constitution under King Talal I which prohibited discrimination based on race, religion, or language and made work and education opportunities available as possible.

Legislative power rests with a National Assembly and the king. The king is supportive of the trend toward greater participation by outsiders in the governing process. The National Assembly is composed of two houses: the Senate and the House of Representatives. Senators are appointed by the king to a term of four years, but may be reappointed. Their number is one half the number of members of the House of Representatives.

The House of Representatives contains eighty seats. Representatives are elected for a four-year term by secret ballot in a general direct election. There are provisions for the king to dissolve the House.

Normally the king would call the National Assembly into its three-month session on November 1. That date can be postponed. The king has the power to dissolve the Assembly before its three-month session is up or he can extend it for a total of six months. The House and Senate act by majority vote. Sessions are public, except when the government or five members request a closed meeting.

Jordan is a hereditary monarchy following the male descent from the dynasty of King Abdullah Bin al Hussein. The king comes of age on his eighteenth lunar year. If a minor is king, the powers are exercised by a regent or a council. If the king is absent or ill, his powers are in the hands of a deputy or a council appointed by the king, or if the king cannot act, by the Council of Ministers.

The king takes an oath to respect the constitution and to be loyal to the country. He approves and promulgates laws, declares war, negotiates peace, and signs treaties. Treaties must be approved by the National Assembly. The king is the commander-in-chief of the navy, army, and air force. He appoints the prime minister and the members of the Senate. He must confirm any death sentence ordered.

A Council of Ministers is made up of the prime minister and the ministers who are responsible for the executive functions of government. Ministers may not be members of any company, receive a salary from any company, or participate in a financial act of trade. The Council of Ministers is responsible to the House of Deputies for matters of policy. Ministers may speak in either the House or the Senate and may vote in the House if they are members. If the House of Representatives rejects the ministers by a two-thirds vote, the ministers must resign. Every new Council of Ministers must present its policy program to the House and ask for a vote of confidence.

The judicial system involves a number of different courts. Most cases would begin in one of the fourteen Magistrates' Courts with jurisdiction limited to small amounts of money and fines or in one of the seven Courts of First Instance. In the latter court, three judges sit in felony trials, while only two judges decide cases of misdemeanors or civil matters. The next level, the Court of Appeal, is a three-judge court. The highest is the Court of Cassation. For most appeals only five judges sit, but for very important cases all seven judges will hear the arguments.

Religious courts decide matters pertaining to marriage, divorce, alimony, inheritance, guardianship, wills, and related family or personal matters. For the Muslims these matters are decided in the Shari'a Court by a single judge applying Islamic law. For the Christians the Ecclesiastical Courts, usually composed of three judges applying Canon Law, rule on matters for the Eastern Orthodox, the Greek Melkites, the Roman Catholics, and the Protestants. In case there is a conflict between the Religious Courts or between the Religious Courts and the Civil Courts, a special tribunal of three judges is appointed by the president of

The Abu Darwish Mosque in Amman was built with alternating patterns of black and white stone.

the Court of Cassation to decide which court has jurisdiction. Where the dispute involves persons of different religions, the Civil Courts have jurisdiction.

RELIGION

While Jordan has a Christian minority and a smaller number of Shiite Muslims, about 95 percent of the population are Sunni Muslims. Muslims are expected to perform certain duties that are often called the Five Pillars of Islam.

First and basic is the confession of faith: "There is no God but the one God, and Muhammad is His Prophet." This statement,

If Muslims cannot reach a mosque for prayer (right), they face the holy city of Mecca and pray where they are (left).

called the *shahadah*, is repeated by the believer many times each day in the prayers. There are other ideas such as faith in God's revelations, in angels, and in a last day that Muslims are expected to believe as well.

A second pillar is the ritual prayer, *salat*, five times daily. There is a ritual washing before prayer. From a standing position, Muslims will bow several times from the waist and prostrate themselves with the forehead touching the ground while silently repeating a quotation from the Koran (their holy book) or other appropriate meditation. These prayers may be performed anywhere the Muslims find themselves, but prayer in the building of worship called a mosque is valued.

Friday is the holy day for the Muslims when they have congregational prayers in the mosque led by an *imam*. A sermon may follow, but the imam is the leader of prayers and not a priest. Muslims have direct access to God (Allah in Arabic). Near the mosque is usually a high tower called a *minaret*, from which the call to prayer is given five times a day. In the past the call was chanted by a person called the *muezzin*. Today, a recording of the call to prayer may be substituted.

Throngs of worshipers in Mecca, Saudi Arabia

The third pillar is the giving of alms, *zakat*, based on a percentage of certain kinds of property. Voluntary contribution above that figure is encouraged also. At first strictly observed, now the practice may not be followed as carefully.

Fasting during the month of Ramadan, *sawm*, is the fourth pillar. Fasting begins at daybreak and lasts until sundown. Eating, drinking, and smoking are prohibited during this period. Since Ramadan is calculated by a lunar calendar, the month can fall at different times of the year as measured by the sun. During the summer, it can be a real test. The ending of Ramadan is celebrated with a great feast, the *Eid al-Fitr*, one of the most important Muslim festivals.

The fifth pillar is the pilgrimage to Mecca called the *hajj*. Every adult Muslim who is able to do so is expected to go on the pilgrimage at least once in a lifetime. The pilgrims wear special dress and go through special ceremonies lasting several days. The ending is celebrated in the second great festival, the *Eid al-Adha*, or Festival of the Sacrifice, in remembrance of Abraham's obedience in his willingness to sacrifice his son.

The revelations of God to Muhammad are contained in the Koran, the holy book of Islam. Copies of the Koran are treated with great respect. The Koran is the highest authority for the Muslim in matters of faith and law.

Muslims accord special status to Jews and Christians, and they recognize Jesus, Abraham, Moses, and others as prophets. They believe that the Bible contains God's words, but the human transmission of them has been flawed.

Groups have interpreted the Islamic religion in different ways. The two major divisions are the Sunni and the Shiite. They have different views about the way the successor to Muhammad should be chosen and about the traditions and the law that should govern the faithful.

EDUCATION

Until 1921, education was limited to the religious or Koranic schools where the Koran was memorized by the students. After 1921, public and private education was established with a broader focus. Education is considered a very important part of Jordan's growth. In a land that lacks some of the natural resources of the oil-rich Near East, it is even more vital to see that human resources are cultivated.

A child begins the first grade of elementary school when five years, eight months old. Classes are taught in Arabic. A study of English begins in fifth grade. After six years of elementary school,

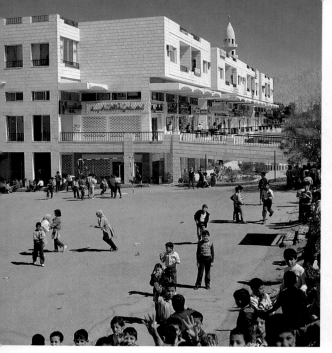

Elementary school students enjoying a break (left)
and applying themselves in the classroom (right)

most students go on to a three-year preparatory school. Following
that, secondary school with a three-year term provides three types
of education: general, vocational, or comprehensive. At the end of
this course, students must take a general secondary examination.
Those who pass may continue their education at one of the four
universities at Amman, Irbid, and Muta or in community colleges.
Of course they also may go to foreign universities. The Jordanian
universities offer degrees in the arts, sciences, education, business,
medicine, agriculture, and engineering. The community colleges
provide two-year programs. The ministry of education controls
twelve of these community colleges and supervises twenty-two
more run by private groups. Seven other colleges are under the
control of other government agencies such as the ministries of
health and social development, the armed forces, the department
of statistics, and the central bank of Jordan.

Elementary education is free and compulsory. At the secondary
level, textbooks are provided at cost. In 1985, 8 percent of the total

 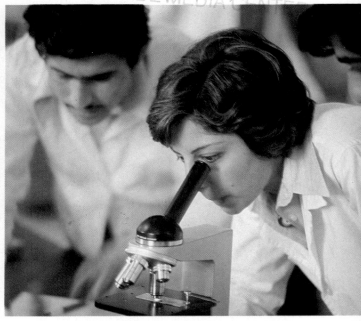

University students studying architecture (left) and science (right)

national budget went to the ministry of education. In 1980, there were eighty libraries run by towns and community societies. There has been a program to distribute children's books throughout the countryside.

The efforts of Jordan to improve literacy and to establish universities providing quality education have been admired by other Near Eastern countries facing the same problems. The refugees who have seen land and other wealth destroyed place a high value on education that cannot be taken away once gained.

THE ARTS

Showcase for the arts and crafts of Jordan is the annual Jerash Festival of Culture and Arts. It has been held in July since it was founded in 1981. The ancient amphitheater from Greek and Roman days in the town of Jerash has been restored and can seat over five thousand people with a 262-foot (80-meter) wide staging

Rug weaving is a traditional Jordanian craft.

area. The idea for the festival was backed by Queen Noor and has the support of the royal family.

The Jordanian National Handicraft Project is another organization that is helping to preserve the many beautiful traditional crafts. Rugs, pottery, jewelry, embroidery, musical instruments, glass, copper, and brass ware are some of the products being encouraged, both in order to preserve the skills necessary for these handcrafted works of art and also in order to increase the work opportunities for the artisans.

While Western music is appreciated in Jordan, Arab music with its complex rhythm patterns, absence of harmony, and use of a scale with the smallest possible interval (the quarter-tone) is still the most popular. Singers of this Arabic music have a following similar to Western stars. Since the vocal element is more important than the instrumental background, the instrumentalists

A shepherd playing a gasabah

usually perform only as an accompaniment to the singer. The instruments usually included in such an ensemble are the *ud* (a stringed instrument), *ganun* (a type of harp), *gasabah* (a short cane flute), *duff* (a tambourine), and *durbakkah* (an earthenware drum). Folk music includes traditional pieces handed down within the tribes as well as contemporary songs improvised for celebrations.

Art that represents animals or humans is not considered proper under one interpretation of Muslim tradition. However, even in the first century of Islam, the pictures in the desert palaces show that this idea has had its exceptions. Since World War II there has been an interest in painting, and Jordan has produced artists who have exhibited their works. Because of the objection to representational art, calligraphy has been much prized. When a movie was to be made of the life of Muhammad, there was much concern in the Islamic community about how this could be done

*The King Abdullah Mosque displays the
use of decorative arts in Muslim architecture.*

without picturing the prophet. The producers solved the problem by having the story told through the eyes of Muhammad so there was no need to picture the prophet.

Literature is the creative form that historically has been the most highly valued of the arts. The Arabs have a significant literature of poetry, legend, and religious stories. The poet is highly respected in Jordan. Jordanian writers have used both classical and new forms of literature.

If a period of peace prevails in the country, the Jordanian contribution to the arts can be expected to grow. The country's traditional art forms can be expected to find worldwide appreciation as the country has more contacts with international markets and its artists become better known.

Chapter 6

IRRIGATED AGRICULTURE, PHOSPHATES, AND A STELLAR AIRLINE

War has upset the Jordanian economy a number of times in recent history. In 1948, Jordan acquired the West Bank territory and greatly increased its population. Then in the 1967 War, that territory was taken over by Israel. However, approximately 300,000 persons fled into Jordan. The loss of that territory meant the loss of some of the best farmland and the tourist attractions of the Holy Land that brought in valuable foreign exchange. While other Arab countries responded with aid to Jordan to help with the refugee problem, the nation faced severe economic conditions.

The war between Iraq and Iran that began in September 1980 brought a closer alliance between Jordan and Iraq as war supplies were funneled to Iraq through Aqaba. Foreign aid and the money sent into the country by Jordanians working abroad helped to give Jordan a period of remarkable growth. From 1974 to 1984, the East Bank region's gross domestic product expanded in real terms at an average annual rate of more than 8 percent—one of the highest growth rates in the world.

However, the targets of the 1981-85 development plan were not met because of a lack of funds. Aid from Arab states declined. The world oil glut caused a decline in the economies of the Arab oil states. Workers abroad were affected, and the money they sent home declined. The decline in trade with Iraq was somewhat offset by an increase in trade with Egypt.

To deal with the economic decline, the prime minister banned imports of luxury items, cut expenditures, and restricted transactions in other currencies. However when he raised the price of fuel and other basic commodities except for bread, sugar, and rice, riots broke out in April 1989. The price increases were part of the economic program required by the International Monetary Fund to enable Jordan to renegotiate its $6.5 billion foreign debt (later revealed to have been 20 percent higher—or closer to $8.2 billion). The prime minister was replaced when charges of mismanagement and corruption surfaced, but the new administration still had to deal with the economic problems such as increasing unemployment. Managing to provide basic government services to low-income families while trying to improve new light industries and tourist attractions would not be easy.

AGRICULTURE

Fluctuation in rainfall is still a crucial factor to success in the agricultural sector of the economy. From 1974 to November 1979 the country experienced a harsh drought. Then the November rains turned out to be the heaviest in thirty-five years. In 1984 the nation experienced the most severe drought in thirty-seven years. Of course, irrigation plans are of the utmost importance in this kind of situation. The best arrangements often involve the

The East Ghor Canal (left) has supplied water for irrigation to help crops such as tomatoes flourish in the Jordan Valley (right).

building of expensive dams. Ninety-two percent of Jordan's land that is able to be cultivated is now rainfed only.

Agriculture employs a little over 7 percent of the border labor force—down from 18 percent in 1979. The net import of food commodities has risen. Agricultural production has increased largely because of the growth in dairy products, poultry, and vegetables.

The Jordan Valley has its own development plan because the irrigation system and its more favorable subtropical climate allow for the production of high-value crops. Intensive farming has permitted large increases in production of fruits and vegetables. The irrigation system was greatly damaged by the Israeli bombardment in 1967. Now the system has been repaired, and the King Talal Dam and other projects have been constructed to increase the land under irrigation. The Jordan Valley Development Plan included providing transportation links, grading and marketing centers, schools, health clinics, and

Cultivation of seedlings in a plastic greenhouse

housing. By using plastic tunnels, greenhouses, and drip irrigation and by introducing better strains of seed, inorganic fertilizers, and mechanization, farmers have increased production.

Attention also is being given to other parts of the country where production is mostly in wheat and barley. Grain storage has been improved. While production varies greatly depending on rainfall, there has been a general increase.

Between 1973 and 1986, the United States Agency for International Development estimated that vegetable production increased by 149 percent, fruit by 546 percent, and field crops by 88 percent. A government-owned public marketing organization was established to deal with marketing problems. Into the 1990s the government continued to subsidize basic food commodities such as rice, milk, and sugar.

Phosphate mines provide Jordan's main export item.

INDUSTRY AND MINING

Compared with its oil-rich neighbors, Jordan is not rich in natural resources. Its manufacturing industry is comparatively recent and is centered around Amman. About 65 percent of all factories produce food products or clothing, but the major income producers are phosphate extraction, cement manufacture, and petroleum refining.

Phosphate production is the main export item. At the end of the 1980s, the phosphate rock industry accounted for at least 47 percent of the country's export earnings. Expansion of this industry has been a major part of the nation's development plans. Other resources that may be promising in the future are uranium, vanadium, petroleum, copper, gypsum, manganese, sand of glass quality, and clays and feldspar for ceramics. Foreign investors are interested in companies for the production of ceramics and sheet glass and for the extraction of potash deposits in the Dead Sea. A plant was built near Zarqa to obtain silver from waste products.

Phosphate has been mined at several locations in Jordan. Future efforts will probably be concentrated on a major new low-cost mine at al-Shidiyya southeast of Ma'an. Work has begun on constructing a railway from the mine to the port at Aqaba, and a phosphate fertilizer plant has been established south of Aqaba.

To meet its energy needs, Jordan must import crude petroleum from Saudi Arabia and Iraq. The country's only oil refinery at Zarqa has increased capacity that handles its imports as well as the small amount produced in Jordan's Hamrah oil field. With oil import costs going up with increased usage and higher prices, Jordan is exploring other possibilities within its own boundaries such as using the shale oil deposits, exploring for new sources of oil, and tapping into newly discovered natural gas reserves at al-Rishah near the Iraqi border.

Cement plants at Fuhais and Rashadiyya helped to meet the needs of the construction industry and provide for exports to Egypt. Gypsum reserves have been discovered that will benefit the cement industry. Sulfuric acid plants are on the drawing board.

Aqaba has the potential for an important fishing industry. Port facilities there are undergoing expansion plans. The 1994 peace treaty includes joint customs and a free-trade zone for Aqaba. Also, Aqaba has a thermal power station.

The government is interested in encouraging new industries. In order to decentralize industrialization, the government established three zones: (a) Amman and its suburbs, (b) other major cities, and (c) the rest of the country. In order to get new plants established away from Amman, the minimum capital asset requirement for companies was three times as much in zone a as for zone c. Plans for industrial areas were made for the region around Irbid and the Ma'an-Aqaba area. Export industry has been encouraged. Duty-free zones have been established at the Queen Alia International Airport and the port of Aqaba. There also are free trade zones at Zarqa and at Ramtha on the Syrian border. Economic cooperation is stressed in the 1994 treaty.

Water supply is a major problem for Jordan. Pumping water from the Euphrates River and the Jordan River has been explored. Searches for groundwater, the building of dams, and investigations of desalinization are ongoing. The 1994 treaty recognized a mutual right to river waters and cooperation to alleviate shortages.

TRANSPORTATION

Rail links, port modernization, road construction, and a ferry route to the Egyptian port of Nuweiba have helped ransportation problems. Under the 1994 treaty negotiations continue for building a highway between Egypt, Israel, and Jordan. The old Hijaz railway that ran from Ma'an north to Damascus, Syria, may never be rebuilt completely. However, it is exciting to railway buffs as a tourist feature that travels past train cars derailed by Lawrence of Arabia.

The most exciting development story in the transportation field is the Royal Jordanian Airlines. In 1962 King Hussein asked Ali Ghandour, later chairman of the line, to formulate plans for an airline. Ghandour was an engineer by profession and had been a vice-president of the Lebanon International Airways. Plans were approved, and on December 8, 1963, the new line came into existence. The first flight took off for Beirut with the line

A Royal Jordanian airplane

expanding to Cairo, Egypt, and Kuwait within a week and to Jeddah, Saudi Arabia, within a month. Now the airline has many jets that serve about forty cities on four continents.

When Jordan lost the West Bank, the company had difficulty raising capital. The king changed the status of the corporation from private to government-owned so that equipment could be purchased and new routes opened up. The line offers nonstop service to the United States and plans to expand to more nations. Now the corporation is the first state company scheduled to be returned to private ownership.

Royal Jordanian developed an air freight, an air taxi, and a flying ambulance service. It has a catering service that prepares about ten thousand meals a day. It runs a duty-free shop at the Queen Alia International Airport, a training center, and even its own art gallery promoting works by local and international artists.

The airline provides tourism offices abroad in its sales offices. It has financial and management interest in hotels and has developed package tours in Jordan.

Technical skills have been taught to Jordanians encouraged through the operation of the airline. The company established an Air Academy to provide training for flight, engineering, maintenance, and computer skills. In 1985 the academy was designated the Regional Technical Center for the Middle East by the International Air Transportation Association. Ghandour hoped to have an air university to train personnel for the whole Middle East area. The king, who frequently pilots his own planes, was an enthusiastic backer of the plan.

FINANCE

In 1950 Jordan had only two commercial banks and a currency board with responsibility for limited monetary policy. By 1992, the country had twenty commercial banks (ten Jordanian-owned) with nearly 343 branches in cities and villages throughout the nation. In addition, there are specialized credit institutions for the fields of housing, industry, agriculture, and local government. A stock exchange, investment and insurance firms, and savings and pension funds also exist. The Central Bank of Jordan was established in 1964 to replace the currency board. That bank issues and regulates currency, manages reserves and control of foreign exchange, takes charge of revenues and expenditures of government ministries and departments. It is banker to licensed banks and specialized credit institutions, supervises and regulates banking activities, and plays an important role in economic development.

During boom times many new houses and apartments were built in Amman.

In 1986 the government lifted most restrictions preventing non-Jordanian Arabs from investing in the country, to encourage private capital to come to Jordan. International Monetary Fund renegotiations of foreign debt made development plans difficult.

In 1993 Israel and the Palestine Liberation Organization (PLO) reached certain peace accords which could affect Jordan's economy. Two-thirds of Jordan's subjects are of Palestinian origin, who could choose to remain loyal to the PLO. Palestinians also dominate Jordanian business. The subsequent 1994 Israeli-Jordanian Peace Treaty is a comprehensive treaty that settled disputes over land and water rights and agreed to cooperation in diplomatic and economic matters including tourism, energy, environment, and drug control, to secure harmony among all states involved.

Chapter 7

THE JORDANIANS: BEDOUIN AND CITY DWELLER

In the new yet old country of Jordan, citizens are faced with change and opportunities. While honoring the Arab-Bedouin ideals, the Jordanians are incorporating new technology and styles that make life easier and safer for them. The choices that they must make may increase their appreciation for what is uniquely Jordanian while they adapt what they want from other cultures.

ETHNIC AND RELIGIOUS GROUPS

The ethnic majority of the population is Arab. The typical Arab has a thin face with a thin curved nose, dark brown or black hair, black or dark brown eyes, and a dark complexion. Usually the people are slender and of medium to short stature. The Palestinian refugees from the West Bank and inhabitants of the Jordan Valley are slightly taller, with a heavy build, and have a broader head. The difference may have resulted from the influx of other races with the frequent invasions of that territory. The Palestinians have been traditionally city and town dwellers with an interest in business and trade.

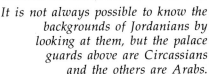

It is not always possible to know the backgrounds of Jordanians by looking at them, but the palace guards above are Circassians and the others are Arabs.

The largest minority is the Circassians who came from Russia when the Ottoman Turks resettled them in Jordan in the late nineteenth and early twentieth centuries. They are tall, light skinned, often with blond hair and blue eyes, and have adopted Western-style dress. Also, they are abandoning their traditional language, Cherkess, in order to adopt Arabic. Many Circassians are in the armed forces. One elite unit made up of this group has special uniforms reflecting their Caucasus origin with black fur hats, long coats, riding boots, and long daggers. They are a royal honor guard. Intermarriage with Arabs is not unusual since these people are Sunni Muslims. Circassian traditions include inheritance of all the property by the oldest son and a ceremonial stealing of the bride.

The Chechens, also known as the Shishans, are similar to the Circassians. They also come from the Caucasus, but they are Shiite

An Arab prays in a Muslim cemetery. The Gethsemane Catholic Church is in the background, in the Old City of Jerusalem, which has religious sites that are holy to Islam, Christianity, and Judaism.

rather than Sunni Muslims. They arrived in the late nineteenth century and their language and some customs differ from those of the other Caucasians. Among the Chechens, all men have equal rights and social status.

Christian groups date back to the time of early Christianity. They represent different denominations, the largest being the Greek Orthodox whose worship is conducted in both Greek and Arabic. A smaller group split from the Orthodox to become the Greek Catholics, under the leadership of the pope in Rome. Protestant missionary efforts have resulted in a small number of followers of this branch. The Christians tend to identify with their Muslim counterparts as either Palestinians or East Bank Jordanians and some, like their Arab neighbors, are organized along tribal lines. Nevertheless, because of church organization, schools run by the churches, and their minority status, Christians have tended to work together in communities. They are represented out of proportion to their numbers in business and banking.

Generally the Christians and Muslims get along well together. They visit socially and attend each other's religious ceremonies. However, intermarriage is rare. There are some strains in their relationships. The Christians have been concerned at the imposition of a national curricula on Christian schools as well as state schools. Moreover, though Christians have held high positions in the government, there are some offices such as prime minister that as a practical matter are closed to them. While the constitution proclaims freedom and equality for all, it also decrees Islam as the official religion. There are differences between the two groups in their attitudes toward the family, with only one wife permitted by the Christians and greater freedom given to Christian women.

THE FAMILY

The family is very important in Jordan. The behavior of an individual reflects on the entire clan. The family feels an obligation to support and protect its members. It is the father's line that determines the composition of the family. When a woman marries, her children belong to the family of their father. The father is the authority for the others. All persons with the same family name may consider themselves descendants from some remote ancestor.

Under traditional Arab law, an unmarried male has the legal right to marry his closest cousin, normally his father's brother's daughter. That cousin may not marry someone else without his

A Christian family

permission. If there is no first cousin on his father's side, other cousins are still preferred. These customs still have a following and as a result the family is bound together even tighter. The spokesman for the family will often be the one to deal with outsiders in political and social matters as well.

At first these family groupings existed in the locality where the family resided. As members of the family in modern times have moved away for business and educational reasons, these persons have tended to marry outside their family units, seeking spouses of a similar educational and social background.

Religious laws regulate marriage and divorce. Multiple marriages are permitted to the Muslim male, although they are not very common. Also, divorce is easier for Muslims though not frequent because of the financial burden involved. The price of a bride is high for the man, and under most marriage contracts, he must make an even higher separation settlement.

TRIBES

From the history of Jordan, it can be seen that tribes have
played an important role. Family units grouping together in a
territory may be joined to a larger unit consisting of other family
groupings. There is a vertical leadership organization as well, so
that the power structure is more like a pyramid in shape made up
of smaller pyramids. Subgroups consolidate power and leadership.
In turn they have a leader at still higher levels. At the highest
levels are tribal confederations made up of tribes that have joined
together over the centuries for various purposes.

Tribal lines are somewhat variable, with splits and
consolidations possible. At times of election for political offices in
Jordan, members of a tribe may be influenced by their loyalty to
their group.

LIVING PATTERNS

Nomadic, seminomadic, semisedentary, and sedentary patterns
are found in Jordan. The true nomadic type is represented by the
Bedouin who depend mostly on camels for their wealth and who
live in black, goat-hair tents rather than in permanent homes.
Usually the tribe or section of the tribe has definite winter and
summer camping grounds and moves back and forth to these
areas.

The seminomadic people may own camels but depend mostly
on sheep and goats. They live in one area and move only short
distances. Both the nomads and the seminomads may plant some
grain crops.

The semisedentary tribes rely more on crops and practice

Some Bedouin live in black, goat-hair tents (above). Seminomadic people may own camels, but also depend on sheep and goats (above right). Rugs are the chief decor in Bedouin tents (right).

animal husbandry. Only part of their group moves with the sheep and goats to new pastures while the rest stay with their fields.

The sedentary groups are either farmers who depend on their crops for most of their money with perhaps one herder taking care of their animals, or they are village and city dwellers with business interests there.

There has been a definite shift from the nomadic style to the sedentary way of life as the Bedouin have settled in villages and more people are moving out of agricultural occupations into jobs associated with urban areas. Moreover, even in the early days of the British mandate, the Bedouin population was probably no more than 40 percent. However, politically and culturally the Bedouin are influential. The significant numbers of Bedouin in the army in elite units and at the officer level are important. Moreover, the customs and ideas such as hospitality, loyalty, and honor are admired by all Jordanians as part of their national

Bedouin women

heritage. The introduction of literacy, health, and nutrition projects together with the replacement of camels with trucks are bringing about changes in the typical life-style of the Bedouin.

The villagers in Jordan call themselves *fellahin,* "farmers." They have moved out of tents into permanent homes. Often they are proud of their fine horses. Family and tribal loyalty is still very important, but economic factors are now playing a stronger role in determining policy and leadership. Some villages are now focused on manufacturing or mining rather than on agricultural crops. Schools and clinics have provided new services to the villages, but supplying uncontaminated drinking water remains a problem for many places.

The urban areas of Jordan—especially the capital of Amman—are like boom towns. People have crowded into the cities for their resources and cultural advantages. Refugees have preferred to

Jordanians celebrating King Hussein's fiftieth birthday

settle in these areas. Housing has been a problem. Several generations of families have had to stay together because of the shortages. It is in the cities that the contrast between the fancy homes and cars of the wealthy and the overcrowded housing of the poor is most evident. In the countryside, wealth is handled more discretely.

DRESS

Western dress is common in Jordan. Even jeans may be seen on the streets—but no shorts because they are not considered modest. Today, more Muslim women are dressing conservatively, covering their heads and arms.

The traditional dress is still seen. Both men and women wear an ankle-length, free-flowing cotton gown called the *thawb*. Over this

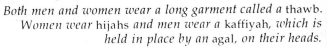

Both men and women wear a long garment called a thawb. *Women wear* hijahs *and men wear a* kaffiyah, *which is held in place by an* agal, *on their heads.*

garment, men may wear a sleeveless coat of cotton, wool, or camel hair called the *abah*. In summer months this garment may be made of silk. Sometimes in villages and cities the thawb is covered by a Western-style suit jacket. The scarf that men wear on their heads is called a *kaffiyah*. It is a white or checkered pattern cloth of cotton that is folded in a triangle and placed on the head so that the middle point hangs in the back and the two ends come over the shoulders. It is held in place by a coil of black cord that is named the *agal*. This head covering is very practical because it protects the head and neck from the sun and can be wrapped around the face to give protection in a sandstorm. Sometimes the abah and the kaffiyah are embroidered with gold.

Women wear a long-sleeved, ankle-length dress, called a *kaftan*, in place of an abah. It is often embroidered with traditional family patterns and worn by city women for formal evening dress because of its beauty.

Ready-made clothing is available, but handcrafted items are still prized. Women often knit and crochet items for their family and to sell to others.

Strong, thick coffee is served in very small cups.

FOOD

Jordanians have a light breakfast and supper. Their main meal is lunch. The most common meat is lamb. Pork is forbidden to Muslims. Fresh vegetables, such as tomatoes and olives, and potatoes, rice, and Arabic bread would complete a meal. Coffee is always available, strong and thick. It is served in very small cups. The guest is expected to take at least one cup, but not more than three.

A Bedouin feast, known as a *mensef*, is a special occasion. A

Guests help themselves at a mensef

whole sheep is killed, skinned, and cooked. Parts of the sheep are put on a huge platter of rice with the head placed in the middle. A sauce prepared from dry yogurt is poured over the dish, and meat is topped with chopped parsley and fried nuts. The honored guest may be presented with the eyes of the sheep, a delicacy. Traditionally the meal is eaten with only the right hand. Mensef also may be prepared with a goat or camel. In the towns, a chicken is commonly substituted.

There are many other Jordanian dishes that are delicious; however, the most common food is the bread, *khubiz,* and is served at every meal. It is always round and flat. Khubiz is treated with reverence as a gift from God and is never thrown away. Leftover pieces may be placed on a windowsill or ledge for hungry persons to take.

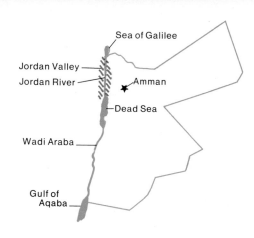

Sea of Galilee

Jordan Valley

Jordan River

Amman

Dead Sea

Wadi Araba

Gulf of Aqaba

Chapter 8

THE SIGHTS AT
THE SITES IN JORDAN

Anyone visiting Jordan will be attracted to the capital city of Amman. Also, the nation boasts many other fascinating cities and places from the Dead Sea to the port of Aqaba, from the ancient city of Jerash to the hidden caravan center of Petra.

AMMAN

This capital city was a mere village when King Abdullah decided to locate his government here in the 1920s. The town has experienced a boom in growth since then and is now home to over one million people.

Amman was inhabited from the early Bronze Age and is mentioned in the Old Testament in connection with David's attack on the city and with prophecies of Amos, Jeremiah, and Ezekiel. The city was then lost from history until Ptolemy II Philadelphus captured it in the third century B.C. and renamed it Philadelphia. It was famous during Greek and Roman times, the early Byzantine period, and the Umayyad Caliphate, after which it lost its importance. Significant archaeological explorations are

Amman is built on six hills. The restored Roman theater (above) was cut into the side of a hill. Hotels, with shops on the ground floor, are found on King Faisal Street (below left), and a merchant's shop displays the kaffiyahs *that are for sale (below right).*

It is busy and noisy in downtown Amman.

being carried out to better understand the long history of this city. The Amman Archaeological Museum contains many items of great importance that have been discovered throughout the country.

Amman also boasts the Jordan Museum of Popular Traditions that houses exhibits of traditional dress, jewelry, and utensils and a Folklore Museum that portrays the traditional life of the Bedouin. Both of these institutions are housed in wings of the ancient Roman theater built in the second or third century A.D. The theater that was built against the slope of a hill can seat six thousand people and is said to have an almost perfect orientation for minimizing the sunlight in the eyes of the spectators. The theater is still used for concerts and outdoor performances.

The Hussein Sports City has a large stadium seating twenty-five thousand. Also there are soccer and track fields; three large swimming pools; tennis, badminton, volleyball, basketball and squash courts; a gymnasium; and a dormitory for visiting teams.

The campus of the University of Jordan

A Palace of Culture shaped to suggest a huge Bedouin tent has a twenty-five-hundred-seat auditorium for use for dramatic, musical, and social events as well as providing space for conferences and conventions. The Sports City also has a public garden with some thirty thousand trees. The National Martyrs Memorial to the Unknown Soldier has a small military museum with exhibits of modern history, tracing the exploits of the great Arab revolt and the modern military history of Jordan.

Sports are popular in Jordan. However, the most common game is probably backgammon, often played outdoors and around the coffeehouses that are gathering places.

The old shopping center called the *souk* is an important stop for purchasing Jordanian handcrafts.

Just north of Amman is the campus of the University of Jordan with its enrollment of over twelve thousand. The 300-acre (121-hectare) campus has some twenty-six buildings with more construction planned.

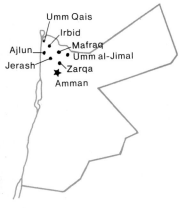

Excavation of the ruins of Jerash, which is thought to have been a city of about fifteen thousand people, began in the 1920s.

NORTH OF AMMAN

Jerash, famous for its Roman and Byzantine ruins, is twenty-nine miles (forty-seven kilometers) north of the capital. Although the temples and the Street of Columns are impressive sights that bring tourists to a sound and light presentation of the city's history, it is estimated that 90 percent of the ancient city is still buried. Jerash is also the site of the arts festival held each summer.

Ajlun, north and west of Jerash, has been developed as a weekend resort center. Its twelfth-century Arab castle gives a spectacular view of the Jordan Valley from Mount Hermon in the north to the Dead Sea on the south. The castle was built as a defense against the Crusaders, but was later partially destroyed by the Mongols. Not far away is the Debbin National Park, a national forest that is enjoyed by the Jordanians as a place to picnic and relax in one of the few wooded areas in their country.

The Nymphaeum (above)
was the ornamental
fountain of Jerash,
with a temple
dedicated to the Nymphs
(mythological maidens).
The Street of
Columns (left) is
paved with the
original stones.
Ruts worn by Roman
chariots can still be seen.

Irbid, northwest of Jerash, is a fast growing industrial area and home to the new Yarmouk University. It is the administrative center of a very fertile area.

Umm Qais, near the Syrian border, is the ancient city of Gadara that was one of the most important members of the Decapolis. Archaeological ruins are found on a hill that affords a wonderful view of the Sea of Galilee, the Yarmouk River Valley, and the Golan Heights. Many significant ancient ruins are found here and at nearby Pella. Excavations at Pella may uncover ruins as extensive as those at Jerash.

Northeast of Amman is Ruseifa, which was one of the main centers for phosphate mining. Nearby, Zarqa is an important industrial center of Jordan. It was the home of the Arab Legion. Mafraq is located in a desert of black basalt. This administrative center started with the building of an oil pipeline. At present the area does not support a large population, but there is evidence at Umm al-Jimal of many ancient buildings of Roman and Byzantine date. An ancient water system from a dam across a wadi may give a clue as to how the population survived.

EAST OF AMMAN

Out in the desert to the east are the castles built by the Umayyad leaders and local Jordanian rulers. They are not large enough to be fortresses to guard frontiers. Most probably they were hunting lodges or stopping points for caravans on trading routes from Yemen, Saudi Arabia, India, or Afghanistan. They are significant as examples of early Islamic secular architecture and art. The paintings are of special interest because of their portrayal of camels and local tradesmen. One ceiling, at Qasr Amra on the

Kharana Castle in the desert near Amman is thought to have been built for defense purposes in the eighth century.

Amman-Azraq road, even has the stars of the zodiac on a hemispherical surface. Some of the desert castles now are easily reached along the new highway linking Amman and Baghdad.

Also out in the desert is the Shaumari Wildlife Reserve near a wetlands section in the Azraq area. Here the only permanent freshwater spring-fed pools in the 12,000 square miles (31,080 square kilometers) of desert that surround it are important resting areas for birds during the migration season. As many as 188 different species have been counted during a week. Zoos are working with the Jordanians to reintroduce rare animals such as the four Arabian oryx of the antelope family that were born in the San Diego Zoo.

WEST OF AMMAN

Two roads lead from Amman down to the Jordan River Valley. Although there are no large cities now along the river, it is here

It is impossible to sink in the Dead Sea.

that are found some of the earliest sites where humans lived together. The region now includes a fertile agricultural area.

The Dead Sea is one of the big attractions south and west of Amman. Because of the mineral salts (33 percent) in the water, the sea contains no animal life except swimmers who find it almost impossible to sink and who often are photographed lying on their backs in the water with a coffee cup or newspaper in hand. Of course, when the swimmers come out of the water they have to wash off the coating of salt that they have acquired. A more practical use for the Dead Sea is the large potash reclamation project through a solar evaporation system at Safi on the southern end of the Dead Sea.

*Above: Mosaics in Madaba
Right: A father and son view the
promised land from Mount Nebo*

SOUTH OF AMMAN

Two roads lead south from the capital to the southern tip of
Jordan at Aqaba. It takes four hours by the Desert Highway that
follows along the old railroad line passing through Ma'an, an
administrative center. The more scenic route is along the ancient
King's Highway that runs through the biblical kingdoms of
Rabbat-Ammon, Moab, and Edom.

On the King's Highway, Hisban has seen occupation since
the Iron Age. Madaba dates from the middle Bronze Age and is
famous for its mosaics. A museum there preserves some of the
finest examples of this art form. Mount Nebo is claimed to be the
site of the tomb of Moses. Nearby is a fortress that is said to be
where Salome danced for King Herod and had John the Baptist
beheaded.

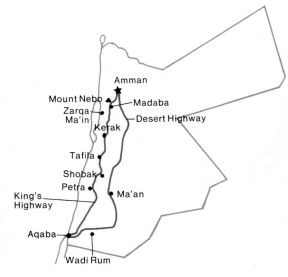

*Nabataean
tombs
at Petra*

A mineral spring at Zarga Ma'in near the Dead Sea is still in use as a health spa. Pools of hot, boiling water come from the hot springs. Dhiban was once the capital of the Moabites, and it is here that the Mesha stele was found. Kerak is the location of the great Crusader castle. There are still many Christian families here, some tracing their roots back beyond the Crusaders to the Byzantine era. Next comes an area west of Tafila and Shobak, which was a mining and smelting section used from the Bronze Age down through the Arab Conquest. Shobak has a Crusader fortress originally built in A.D. 1115.

Petra, the center for the Nabataeans, still attracts many to see the wonders that were once so well hidden by a narrow passage into the city. Famous tombs, a high altar for sacrifices, a Byzantine church, and a Roman theater accommodating three thousand persons can be visited. Here is a tomb with an urn carved from rock that

A few Bedouin families live in Wadi Rum (left), where in the summer the desert (right) becomes extremely hot.

was thought to contain gold treasure. The rocks at Petra under various lighting conditions can look yellow, red, and even purple. Aklat and Beida nearby also are important archaeological sites.

Wadi Rum is a valley to the east of that part of the Desert Highway linking Aqaba and Ma'an between towering rocks on either side. It is the home of several Bedouin tribes. A fort of the desert patrol is there. The scenery was pictured in the film *Lawrence of Arabia*.

Finally, 204 miles (328 kilometers) from Amman is Aqaba, the biblical Eloth. Today, it is a busy port through which passes Jordan's biggest export, phosphate. Because the settlement has been an important stop on trade and pilgrimage routes throughout history, archaeological excavations have turned up significant finds of artifacts, some manufactured as far away as

Sunset at the Gulf of Aqaba

China. The clear water, complex water currents, miles of reefs, numerous shipwrecks, and the large variety of fish make the waters near Aqaba one of the best places for scuba diving. There are at least forty species of coral or fish here that are found nowhere else in the world. Spear fishing and removal of the coral are forbidden. The University of Jordan monitors the impact of construction on the marine life.

A LAND OF CONTRAST

Jordan, the new yet old country, is a land of contrasts. The desert kingdom cares for its marine treasures. This land of history works to make the advantages and opportunities of modern life available to all its citizens.

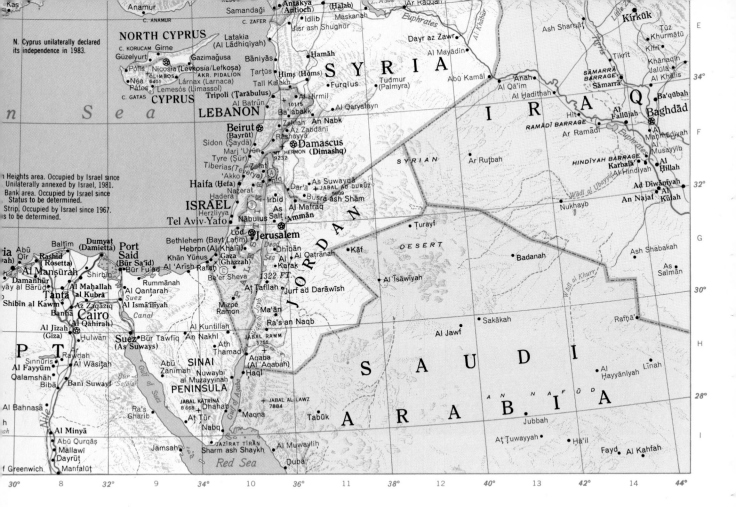

Comprehensive World Atlas, © Copyright 1991 by Rand McNally & Company,
R.L. 91-S-93

MAP KEY

Al Karak (Kerak)	G10	Dhiban	G10
Al Qatranah	G11	Irbid	F10
Al Mafraq	F11	Jabal Ramm (mountain)	H10
Amman	G10	Jurf ad Darawish	G10
Aqaba (Al'Aqabah)	H10	Ma'an	G10
Aqaba, Gulf of	H10	Ra's an Naqb	H10
As Salt	F10	Red Sea	I10
At Tafilah (Tafila)	G10	Suez, Gulf of	H9, I9
Dead Sea	G10	Wadi al Jayb (river)	G10, H10

MINI-FACTS AT A GLANCE

GENERAL INFORMATION

Official Name: Hashemite Kingdom of Jordan

Capital: Amman

Official Language: Arabic

Government: Jordan is a hereditary, constitutional monarchy based on the constitution of 1952. Executive authority is vested in the king and the Council of Ministers. The Council of Ministers, led by a prime minister, is appointed by the king. The king signs and executes all laws, but his veto power can be overridden by a two-thirds vote of both houses of the National Assembly. Legislative power rests with the National Assembly, which is composed of the Senate and the House of Representatives, and the king. Senators are appointed by the king; representatives are elected to four-year terms. The constitution provides for civil, religious, and special courts.

Flag: The flag is a tricolor of black, white, and green horizontal stripes joined at the staff with a seven-pointed white star on a red triangle.

National Anthem: "Al-Salam Al-Malaki" ("The Royal Salute")

Religion: About 95 percent of Jordanians are Sunni Muslims and most of the others (about 4 percent) are Christians, half of whom are Arabic-speaking Greek Orthodox.

Money: The basic unit is the dinar. In November 1994, .68 dinar equaled $1.00 in United States currency.

Weights and Measures: Jordan uses the metric system.

Population: Estimated 1994 population—3,855,000

Cities:	1992 estimates
Amman	1,272,000
Zarqa	605,000
Irbid	385,000

GEOGRAPHY

Highest point: Jabal Rum, 5,755 ft. (1,754 m)

Lowest point: Shore of the Dead Sea, about 1,300 ft. (396 m) below sea level

Mountains: Jordan's terrain consists chiefly of a high desert and steep plateau. Most of it lies between 2,000 and 3,000 ft. (610 and 914 m) over the Rift Valley.

Rivers: The principal river is the Jordan, which flows through Jordanian territory for 97 mi. (156 km). It empties into the Dead Sea. The largest tributary of the Jordan is the Yarmouk River, which forms part of the border with Syria. The Nahr az-Zarqa cuts across the eastern plateau north of Amman.

Climate: The climate is generally arid. The Mediterranean Sea has the greatest climactic influence. Average monthly temperatures in the capital range from 44° to 87° F. (6.6° to 30.5° C), while in the far south they range from 61° to 90° F. (16° to 32° C).

During the summer, spells of hot, dusty winds frequently blow from the southeast off the Arabian Peninsula; these are known as the *khamsin*. Rainfall occurs in the short, cool winters decreasing from 16 in. (41 cm) annually in the northwest toward the Jordan River to less than 4 in. (10 cm) in the south. The valley has an annual rainfall of about 8 in. (20 cm).

Greatest Distances: North to South: 230 mi. (370 km)
East to West: 230 mi. (370 km)

Coastline: 16 mi. (26 km)

Area: 37,738 sq. mi. (97,749 km²)

NATURE

Trees: Trees such as pines, acacias, oaks, and cypress can be found in very small groves or standing alone. Grassland is the common vegetation on the steppe, though there are some shrubs such as the Mount Atlas pistachio and the lotus fruit. In the desert scant vegetation can be found in depressions and on the floors and sides of valleys.

Animals: There is a wide variety of animal life, including wild boar, ibex, gazelles, wild goats, foxes, wildcats, hyenas, wolves, gazelles, mole rats, panthers, and mongooses. Domestic animals include horses, camels, donkeys, mules, sheep, and goats.

Birds: The vulture and the golden eagle are common, as are the pigeon and the partridge. Waterfowl and land birds—especially the stork—are found.

EVERYDAY LIFE

Food: Lunch is the most important meal of the Jordanian day, and lamb the most important meat. Pork is forbidden for Muslims. *Khubiz*, a round and flat bread, is eaten at almost every meal. *Hummus*, a side dish made from a paste of chick-peas, sesame seeds, and garlic, is nutritious and a staple of the Jordanian diet. Yogurt, olives, cheese, and fruits also are basic foods on the Jordanian table. Coffee, strong and thick, is the favorite drink. Special occasions demand a Bedouin feast, or *mensef.* A sheep is killed, skinned, cooked, and served with a sauce made of dried yogurt. Goat, camel, or chicken can be used also.

Housing: The majority of dwellings consist of only one room. The Housing Corporation and the Jordan Valley Authority build low-income housing units. Several generations often are forced to share accommodations. Bedouin live in black, goat-hair tents rather than in permanent dwellings.

Holidays:

> Tree Day, January 15
> Arab League Day, March 22
> Labor Day, May 1
> National Day, May 25
> Coronation Day, August 11
> King's Birthday, November 14

Culture: Literature has traditionally been the most valued art form in Jordan. Arabs have created a significant literature of poetry, legend, and religious stories. Although Islamic art has traditionally been nonrepresentational, since World War II there has been an interest in painting. Calligraphy has been highly prized. The Jordanian National Handicraft Project has been working hard to foster work in rugs, pottery, jewelry, embroidery, copper, and brass. The Jordan Museum of Popular Traditions houses exhibits of traditional dress, jewelry, and utensils. The Amman Archaeological Museum contains the fruits of many archaeological explorations. Arab music is still the most popular, though Western music is appreciated more and more. Folk music includes traditional tribal melodies as well as contemporary works improvised for holidays and celebrations.

Sports and Recreation: The Hussein Sports City has a large stadium that seats 25,000 people. There are also soccer and track fields, swimming pools, and tennis, badminton, volleyball, basketball, and squash courts.

Communication: Jordan has four daily newspapers and four non-dailies. The *Jordan Times* is an English-language daily. There is no prepublication censorship, but the government has the right to confiscate all publications that attack religion, offend national dignity or public morality, or disturb public order. The Hashemite Jordan Broadcasting Service is a department of the Ministry of Communication. The Jordan Radio and Television Corporation began operation in 1972.

Transportation: Good paved roadways link Jordan's major cities and tie them in as well with those in neighboring countries. The Aqaba Railway Corporation operates a new line to the port of Aqaba, and another line goes into Saudi Arabia. Rail links, port modernization, road construction, and a ferry route to the Egyptian port of Nuweiba are among the latest improvements and developments. Royal Jordanian Airlines was founded in 1962 and its jets now serve about forty cities on four continents.

Education: Seventy percent of the population is now literate, one of the highest percentages in the Middle East. Schooling consists of six years of elementary, three years of preparatory, and three years of secondary education. Education is free and compulsory to the age of 14. Most students attend government schools. There are four universities: the State University of Jordan, founded in 1962; Yarmouk University, established in 1976; Muta, which opened in 1981; and the Jordan University of Science and Technology, which opened in the mid-1980s. One-third of the 18-to-22-year-old age group are enrolled in a program of higher education. In addition there are an agricultural training institute, and a number of agricultural secondary schools, as well as institutes for vocational and military training, nursing, and teaching. Many students attend foreign universities.

Health and Welfare: Public welfare in Jordan, as in most Arab countries, has been traditionally provided by family, tribe, and institutions and not by the state. The Islamic alms tax, the *zakat*, however, has been converted into a social welfare tax, and part of its proceeds are used to finance family welfare and rehabilitation of the handicapped. Infectious diseases, except for dysentery and eye infections, have been brought under control. The government operates a comprehensive health program.

ECONOMY AND INDUSTRY

Principal Products:
Agriculture: Tomatoes, figs, lentils, citrus fruits, cucumbers, eggplants, tobacco, olive oil, wheat, barley
Manufacturing: Refined petroleum products, cement, fertilizers
Mining: Potash, phosphate

IMPORTANT DATES

100,000 years ago—Hunters wandered the Jordanian desert

10,000 B.C.—More organized settlements develop

7000 B.C.—Defensive walls are erected near Jericho

4000 to 3600 B.C.—Chalcolithic Period—Several settlements are active

3000 to 2100 B.C.—Early Bronze Age—Civilization seems to develop into small settlements that are eventually destroyed by nomads near Irbid and the Dead Sea area

2000 B.C.—Semitic Amorites settle around Jordan River in area called Canaan

63 B.C.—Romans conquer Jordan

A.D. 313 —Christianity becomes recognized religion of Roman Empire

633—Arabs invade Jordan and Syria

7th Century—Muslim conquest

1099—Jordanian land parceled out to victorious knights of the Crusades

16th Century to 1916—Jordan is part of Ottoman Empire

1916—Sherif Hussein Ibn Ali proclaims Arab revolt against Ottomans with Britain's blessing

1920—Syria and Jordan declared independent of Britain; Britain gets mandate for Palestine; Transjordan is not included

1923—Transjordan proclaimed an autonomous state under League of Nations mandate

1946—Britain recognizes independence of Transjordan with Abdullah as king

1948—State of Israel is born

1949—The kingdom is renamed Jordan; Jordan is left in control of West Bank under United Nations Armistice Agreement

1951—Abdullah is assassinated; Talal is proclaimed king

1952—New constitution is approved, consolidating the king's powers

1953—Hussein becomes king

1955—Jordan is invited to join the United Nations

1955-56—British ties are loosened

1957—Special defense agreement with Britain is dissolved; there is an unsuccessful attempt to unseat Hussein

1958—Egypt and Syria unite to form United Arab Republic; Jordan and Iraq unite into Arab Federation

1960—King Hussein gives speech to United Nations that wins many friends for Jordan in the international community

1967—Jordan signs mutual defense pact with Egypt; Syria, Egypt, and Iraq join Jordan in war with Israel; Jordan suffers many casualties and loses to Israel all the territory it had gained in 1948

1970—Jordanian army attacks Palestinian guerrillas; the hardline Palestinian groups withdraw

1973—Yom Kippur War against Israel; Jordan sends a brigade to fight alongside the Syrian army on the Golan Heights

1974—Arab Summit Conference unanimously recognizes Palestine Liberation Organization (PLO) as sole legitimate representative of the Palestinians

1978—Jordan rejects Camp David accords on Palestinian autonomy

1986—King Hussein embarks on aid program to counter PLO influence on West Bank and forestall influx of Palestinians into Jordan; orders PLO offices to close

1988—Hussein favors establishment of Palestinian state under leadership of PLO; severs legal and administrative ties to West Bank

1989—Economic conditions worsen

1990-91—Jordan supports Saddam Hussein of Iraq in Gulf War

1993—Dr. Abdul-Salam Al Majali, former chief Middle Eastern peace negotiator, is appointed prime minister; King Hussein speculates that elections scheduled for November may be postponed until conditions settle following on peace accords signed between Israel and the PLO and Israel and Jordan; November elections indicate support for King Hussein's peace initiatives when Islamic fundamentalists win a minority of Parliament seats; the first woman legislator is elected

1994—The Israeli-Jordanian Peace Treaty is signed on October 26; fundamentalist groups protest with continued violence; Jordan and the Vatican establish diplomatic ties

IMPORTANT PEOPLE

Abdullah (1882-1951), proclaimed Transjordan an autonomous state under League of Nations mandate; became emir of Transjordan in 1921; grandfather of present king of Jordan

Adadnirari III, king of Assyria from 811-783 B.C. ; conquered East Bank down to Edom

Abu Bakr (c. 573-634), first Muslim caliph

Bin Saud (1880?-1953), Muslim leader and king and founder of Saudi Arabia

Faisal I (1885-1933), king of all Syria, Lebanon, Transjordan, and Palestine in 1920 and king of Iraq from 1921-33

Ali Ghandour (1930-   ), founder, in 1962, of Royal Jordanian Airlines

John Bagot Glubb (1897-1986), British officer, organized desert mobile force known as the Desert Patrol

Hassan (1947-   ), brother of King Hussein and crown prince of Jordan

Sherif Hussein (c. 1854-1931), father of Emir Abdullah and King Faisal I, great grandfather of present king of Jordan

Hussein Ibn Talal (1935-   ), king of Jordan

Muhammad (570-632), prophet of Islam

Muhammad (1940-   ), brother of King Hussein and crown prince of Jordan from 1952-62

Gamel Abdel Nasser (1918-70), president of Egypt

Queen Noor (1951-   ), American-born wife of King Hussein

Frederick G. Peake (1886-1970), known as "Thunder Cloud," a British officer who formed a peacekeeping desert patrol for Transjordan

Saladin (1138-93), sultan of Egypt and Syria; conquered Jerusalem, 1187; renowned for courage and magnaminity

Suleyman (1494 or 1495-1566), called the Magnificent

Talal (1890-1972), king of Jordan from 1951 to 1952

Umar bin Khattab (581?-684), caliph who helped conquer Galilee, the Jordan lowlands, and central and southern Palestine

INDEX

Page numbers that appear in boldface type indicate illustrations

About the Author

Leila Merrell Foster is a lawyer, United Methodist minister, and clinical psychologist with degrees from Northwestern University and Garrett Evangelical Theological Seminary. She is the author of books and articles on a variety of subjects.

Dr. Foster's love of travel began early as she listened to her mother and older sister read aloud travel and adventure stories. As a youngster, she enjoyed the family trips through which she learned geography, geology, history, art, agriculture, and economics in a very pleasant manner.

Dr. Foster also has written *Bhutan* and *Iraq* in the Enchantment of the World series.